Brunch On

By Jim Voltz

Twelve complete brunch menus perfect for elegant but casual
entertaining on the cottage porch or anywhere you enjoy getting
together with friends and family.

Printed in the United States of America

ISBN 978-1-61658-985-1

Illustrated by Chris Patterson
Design and Composition by Composure Graphics

Thanks

Again, I have to thank many old friends and some new ones I have made since writing my first cookbook.

Top of the list goes to Marjorie Elliott and Nancy Myers for their continued support and putting up with a sometimes temperamental chef and friend.

Betsie Hosick and Bob Weber for hosting all the 2009 cooking classes in their home and again volunteering to host the classes in 2010.

Sally Berlin, owner of Crystal Crate and Cargo, for her friendship, advice and support.

Neighbor, friend and artist Chris Patterson for once again creating such wonderful illustrations.

Lee Harper, Director of the Crystal Lake Art Center, for her support of my projects and the culinary arts in general.

Nels Nelson, owner of the East Shore Market, and his wife Karen who have become great friends.

My good friends Tim and Jeri Richardson. Tim provided all the wine suggestions and Jeri provided her wonderful recipe for cottage cheese pancakes.

Priscilla Rush for so scrupulously proofreading the drafts.

All the wonderful friends who have attended my cooking classes.

Thanks to all,

Jim Voltz

Contents

Introduction

What better way to follow my first cookbook, "Dinner on the Porch" than "Brunch on the Porch." Both cookbooks are the result of the many summer parties given on the porch of Sunny Shores, the cottage I share with my best friend Nancy Myers on Crystal Lake near Frankfort, Michigan.

Sunny Shores is one of the smallest cottages on the lake, about 800 square feet, and over a hundred years old but that doesn't keep us from having houseguests and numerous parties throughout the summer. We've done some updating over the years but it is still very much an old cottage. The happiest changes for me were the recent replacement of the little apartment-sized stove with a modern gas stove and the addition of a small apartment-sized dishwasher. We have now maxed out all space and electrical possibilities for the cottage and the kitchen. The porch where we have most of our dinner and brunch parties, and sometimes even store a houseguest or two, remains the same 10 by 24 feet, but we've added windows so we can utilize the area earlier and later in the season without wearing jackets and moving the furniture away from the screens when it rains.

Over the years, we've hosted countless dinner parties for our many friends and family and I've enjoyed them immensely. But quite often I like to mix it up a little and have a brunch instead.

This cookbook consists of twelve of my favorite brunch menus with detailed recipes for each item on the menu, a shopping list, and beverage suggestions. The book demonstrates just how flexible brunch can be with menus that range from the very casual such as my Chili Brunch on page 75 to the very grand and elegant menu consisting of quiche, crab cakes, and a soufflé on page 17. But no matter how elegant the items, they're not difficult to do. I've made the recipes as simple and detailed as possible with tips along the way that will ensure your success. I've easily prepared every item, sometimes for twenty or more guests, in the tiny galley kitchen of our 1910-era cottage.

Of course the key to this success is what I stressed in my first cookbook and continue to stress in all of my cooking classes, "mise en place." "Mise en place" is literally translated as "put in place" and is simply organizing and putting in place all of the ingredients and cooking utensils you will need to prepare a dish before you start cooking. This will ensure you won't have to waste time or become frustrated looking for something while in the middle of preparing a recipe. Another major tip for successful cooking is to read all the recipes in your menu at least twice several days before your party. This will ensure you understand the recipes, have all the ingredients and utensils necessary, and the time required to prepare each dish.

As with my dinner parties, when preparing a brunch, I like to do as much as I can ahead of time. Throughout this book, I've identified items that can be prepared ahead of time and the length of time they will keep. Doing as much as you can before the day of your party will make entertaining so much easier and less stressful. This includes setting the table. Do it the evening before your party. The table setting doesn't need to be anything elaborate. A few fresh flowers, a tablecloth or placemats, un-ironed cotton napkins (no paper napkins please!), and your everyday dishes and glassware will work for just about any brunch.

I like to use local fresh ingredients as much as possible and have found that the Farmers' Markets and family-owned grocery stores offer outstanding produce and specialty items not always found in supermarkets. One of my summer pleasures is to shop the two local farmers' markets held weekly in Frankfort and Elberta. I recommend checking out local farmers' markets in your area if you don't already shop there. I also recommend finding a good wine and specialty market and a good local butcher. Establish a relationship with the owners. They can be a tremendous help and you just might make some great friends.

Brunch to me is anything you prepare and serve between morning coffee and afternoon cocktails. This leaves a wide open option for just about whatever you want to eat and makes for very flexible entertaining. You can do anything from a mid-morning menu consisting of more breakfast type items or move the party to the afternoon and make it a late lunch. This flexibility is one of the main reasons I enjoy hosting a brunch periodically as an alternative to my dinner parties. Guests seem to enjoy the change as well, especially if you can serve brunch on the porch on a warm summer day by the lake.

An original drawing and short story accompany each menu. The drawings are all done by good friend and artist Chris Patterson, and are actual depictions of Sunny Shores and other local sights. The short stories are about people who have been guests on the porch at Sunny Shores or students in my classes with one exception. None of the names have been changed to protect anyone.

"Brunch on the Porch" is dedicated to those who like to prepare something special for friends and family while not having to get up at the crack of dawn and spend hours in the kitchen. I hope you and your guests enjoy these brunches as much as we have at Sunny Shores.

With warm wishes of good meals shared with those you love,

Jim

Bella and Luna Head North

Every spring, my best friend Nancy Myers and I pack up my SUV and head north from Sarasota, Florida to Crystal Lake Michigan where we share the little cottage called Sunny Shores. It's a challenge to round up the two cats, Bella and Luna, and get them in the car; they don't like to travel very well, but maybe that's because of their cramped quarters between my cooking stuff and all of Nan's clothes.

Our first stop is Hendersonville, North Carolina where Nan's sister Shirley Walsh and her husband David always greet us with a fabulous feast of standing prime rib roast, double baked potatoes, Yorkshire pudding, Brussels sprouts, Caesar salad, AND Shirley's latest dessert! On top of this, David cooks fried eggs, bacon, sausage, toast, and coffee for breakfast every morning. We leave Hendersonville with a few extra pounds and a promise from Shirley and David to visit us later in the summer.

As we continue north, our anticipation builds, each of us eager to call out, "I see the lake first!" We can't wait to pull into our little driveway and see Sunny Shores again, knowing that it will soon be full of the family and life-long friends that make this place so special.

This summer I'm going to teach David how to make the frittata from Menu I. I like fried eggs but not every morning.

A New Menu for David
(6 servings)

Beignets served with Coffee

Asparagus Frittata

Homemade Applesauce with Raspberries

Breakfast Sausage Hash

The beignets are going to be the big hit of this menu. Your guests will be standing in the kitchen waiting for them and wanting more. This is an informal but elegant brunch and you can fix the applesauce in advance while the rest of the menu is prepared very quickly and easily. Serve coffee with the beignets and allow a break between them and the rest of the brunch so everyone can savor this New Orleans treat.

Beignets

4 Tbls unsalted butter

1 Tbls sugar

$\frac{1}{2}$ tsp salt

$\frac{1}{2}$ cup flour

4 large eggs

2 tsp pure vanilla extract

2 cups Vegetable oil for deep frying

Powdered sugar for dusting

Asparagus Frittata

8 large eggs

$\frac{1}{2}$ cup heavy cream or half & half as desired

$\frac{1}{2}$ cup grated fresh parmesan cheese (or your choice of any hard cheese)

$\frac{1}{2}$ tsp salt and $\frac{1}{4}$ tsp pepper

10 spears of fresh asparagus

10 cherry tomatoes

2 Tbls olive oil

Applesauce with Raspberries

2 pounds cooking apples of your choice (I like Fuji or Granny Smith but any cooking apple will work)

$\frac{1}{2}$ cup apple juice or cider

1 lemon

1 cinnamon stick

$\frac{1}{2}$ cup sugar

$\frac{1}{2}$ tsp nutmeg

1 pinch of salt

1 pint fresh raspberries

Breakfast Sausage Hash

1 pound breakfast sausage

1 medium yellow onion

1 small red bell pepper

3 medium Idaho potatoes

$\frac{1}{2}$ cup low sodium beef broth

2 Tbls vegetable oil

Salt and pepper to taste

Beignets

1. Preheat a deep fryer or deep-sided frying pan to 365 degrees Fahrenheit or medium high heat with vegetable oil at least 2 inches deep.

2. In a medium sauce pan combine:
   a. 4 Tbls unsalted butter
   b. 1 Tbls sugar
   c. $\frac{1}{2}$ tsp salt
   d. $\frac{1}{2}$ cup water

3. Bring to a steady boil

4. Add $\frac{1}{2}$ cup flour ALL AT ONCE and stir vigorously over medium heat until the mixture comes together and has a little shine to it.

5. Continue cooking and stirring for 2 minutes

6. Transfer to a bowl and add one large egg at a time (total of 4 large eggs) using an electric mixer on medium speed.

7. Add 2 tsp pure vanilla extract and beat for 2 to 3 minutes; the mixture should be smooth and shiny.

8. Dip a tablespoon-sized spoon into the hot oil and then into the batter and immediately drop dough into the hot oil. (Dipping the spoon in the hot oil keeps the batter from sticking to the spoon.)

9. Fry 4 or 5 beignets at a time, approximately 2 minutes per side, until puffed and golden brown on both sides

10. Drain on paper towels and dust with powdered sugar

11. Serve warm with coffee (in New Orleans this would be chicory coffee)

NOTES

Asparagus Frittata

This is basically an open faced omelet which can be served hot, warm or cold. Prepare both the applesauce and the sausage hash before you start the frittata unless you are serving the frittata at room temperature or cold.

1. Preheat the broiler

2. Clean and cut 10 fresh asparagus spears into $\frac{1}{2}$ inch pieces (if using large asparagus you will need to pre-blanch in hot water for 2 to 3 minutes and drain)

3. Cut 10 cherry tomatoes in half, thru the middle, not end to end

4. Preheat a large ovenproof skillet on medium high heat with 2 Tbls olive oil

5. In a large bowl beat 8 large eggs until very frothy. Add:
   a. $\frac{1}{2}$ cup heavy cream or half & half
   b. $\frac{1}{2}$ cup fresh grated parmesan cheese (or your choice of any hard cheese)
   c. $\frac{1}{2}$ tsp salt
   d. $\frac{1}{4}$ tsp pepper
   e. The ten spears of cut asparagus

6. Pour into the preheated pan, stir, reduce the heat to medium and cook until the bottom is set, about 3 to 4 minutes

7. Put the tomato slices on top, open side down

8. Immediately transfer the pan to the broiler (about 2 inches below the heat) and cook for 2 to 3 more minutes until lightly browned

9. Loosen frittata with a spatula and slide onto a serving plate

Applesauce with Raspberries

This is easiest to prepare in advance, but add the raspberries just before serving. (Fresh applesauce will keep nicely for 3 or 4 days in the refrigerator.) You can substitute any berry of your choice for the raspberries. Serve warm or chilled.

NOTES

1. Peel, core and thinly slice 2 pounds of cooking apples (I like Fuji or Granny Smith apples.)

2. In a large saucepan add:
   a. The apple slices
   b. $\frac{1}{2}$ cup apple juice or cider
   c. 1 tsp fresh squeezed lemon juice
   d. 1 cinnamon stick
   e. $\frac{1}{2}$ cup sugar
   f. $\frac{1}{2}$ tsp nutmeg
   g. $\frac{1}{4}$ tsp salt

2. Bring to a boil over medium high heat

3. Reduce heat to medium low, cover and simmer for 20 to 30 minutes until the apples are soft. (time will vary depending on the type of apples used)

4. Remove from heat and discard the cinnamon stick

5. For a chunky sauce, use a fork to smash, for semi smooth use a potato masher, for very smooth use a food processor

6. Let cool and add 1 pint raspberries and stir before serving

Breakfast Sausage Hash

Again, prepare this before the frittata and keep warm in the oven (if you only have one oven take it out and cover before preheating the broiler for the frittata)

1. Peel and dice 3 medium Idaho potatoes (put in salted water if preparing in advance)

2. Dice 1 medium yellow onion

3. Clean and dice 1 small red bell pepper

4. Preheat a large skillet on medium high heat with 2 Tbls vegetable oil

5. Add 1 pound breakfast sausage and crumble with a spatula

6. Add the diced onion and cook on medium high heat until sausage is lightly browned and onion is translucent (do not overcook)

7. Add the red pepper and diced potatoes and cook for 5 minutes

8. Add $\frac{1}{2}$ cup beef broth, cover and simmer on medium heat for 10 minutes, until potatoes are tender

9. Remove cover, add salt and pepper to taste, and cook until broth is gone, about 5 minutes

Serving: Cut the frittata into pie shape wedges and plate with a spoonful of the sausage hash. Serve the balance of the hash in a warm decorative bowl. Serve the applesauce in a decorative bowl with small bowls at each place setting.

Beverages

A light red wine such as a red Sancerre or Chinon, South African Pinotage or domestic Cabernet Franc all go well with this menu. Bloody Marys (see recipe on page 117), a classic brunch beverage, would be another great addition to this meal.

Coffee and fruit juice of choice

Brunch with Julia Child

Julia Child never came to brunch on the porch at Sunny Shores but I got to have brunch at her beautiful home in Hyannis Port, Massachusetts. In the early 1980's, one of my best friends married Julia's goddaughter. Not only was I invited to the wedding, I was also invited to the bridal brunch that Julia was hosting. Oh, happy day. Having been a big fan of Julia and her cooking shows for years, I was particularly looking forward to this; greatly anticipating a wonderful meal prepared by the legendary chef. But it was not to be. It turned out Julia had the entire brunch catered.

I can't complain. I got to spend the better part of the next two days talking about cooking with Julia Child! We became friends over that weekend and stayed in touch for the next several years. Many interesting people have come to brunch on the porch at Sunny Shores. Julia Child was not one of them but oh how I wish she was.

Menu II is the menu I might have served to Julia, knowing her fondness for butter, bacon, and champagne.

Menu II

Remembering Julia
(6 servings)

Vegetable Crudités

Quiche Lorraine

New England Style Crab Cakes

Grand Marnier Soufflé

This is the most elegant menu in the book and I would serve it to a very special group of people, which means anyone you want to impress, including family members. However, it is not the most labor intensive menu and is really quite easy to prepare. Give it a try and sit back and wait for the "oohs and ahs", especially with the Grand Marnier soufflé.

Vegetable Crudités

1 bunch celery

1 bunch carrots

1 bunch small green onions

1 English cucumber

Quiche Lorraine

1 deep 9 inch pastry shell

6 slices regular bacon

5 large eggs (1 for the pastry glaze)

$1\frac{1}{2}$ cups heavy cream or half & half

$\frac{1}{8}$ tsp fresh nutmeg

$\frac{1}{2}$ tsp salt

$\frac{1}{4}$ tsp white pepper

Crab Cakes

1 pound of cooked real crab meat

2 large eggs

4 Tbls mayonnaise

1 small red bell pepper

$1\frac{1}{4}$ tsp Old Bay Seasoning

$\frac{1}{4}$ tsp cayenne pepper

$1\frac{1}{4}$ tsp yellow mustard

$1\frac{1}{2}$ tsp fresh parsley

8 Ritz crackers

1 Tbls vegetable oil

Tartar sauce, optional

Soufflé and Sauce

9 large eggs

$\frac{1}{2}$ pound unsalted butter (2 sticks)

2 Tbls flour

12 oz heavy cream

1 cup sugar

1 bottle Grand Marnier

1 orange

Salt

Vegetable Crudités

Serve the crudités along with your favorite cold brunch drink (see pages 23 and 113 for ideas) as a starter.

1. Clean and cut 3 or 4 stalks of celery into 6-inch long narrow pieces

2. Peel and cut 3 or 4 carrots into 6-inch long narrow pieces

3. Clean one bunch of small green onions and leave whole

4. Peel and cut one English cucumber into 6-inch long wedges

5. Serve on a platter with drinks (no dipping sauce is necessary, the rest of the menu is very rich)

Quiche Lorraine

NOTES

This is a last minute dish, unless you plan to serve it cold

1. Preheat oven to 375 degrees Fahrenheit
2. Brush a deep dish, 9-inch pastry shell with egg yolk glaze (1 egg yolk and 1 tsp water mixed) and bake per directions on package and let cool to room temperature
3. Fry 6 slices of regular bacon until crisp, drain and set aside
4. In a large bowl whisk 4 large eggs until frothy
5. Add the following to the eggs and mix well:
   a. $1\frac{1}{2}$ cups heavy cream or half & half
   b. $\frac{1}{2}$ tsp salt
   c. $\frac{1}{4}$ tsp white pepper
   d. $\frac{1}{8}$ tsp fresh grated nutmeg
6. Crumble the bacon onto the bottom of the pastry crust
7. Pour the egg mixture on top
8. Bake until set, about 25 to 30 minutes
9. Serve warm or at room temperature

New England Style Crab Cakes

I would prepare this recipe through step 4 (up until sautéing) and refrigerate until the quiche goes in the oven.

1. In a large bowl whisk 2 large eggs until frothy and then add:
   a. 4 Tbls good mayonnaise
   b. $1\frac{1}{4}$ tsp Old Bay Seasoning
   c. $\frac{1}{4}$ tsp cayenne pepper
   d. $1\frac{1}{4}$ tsp yellow mustard
   e. $1\frac{1}{2}$ tsp chopped fresh parsley
   f. 8 crumbled Ritz crackers
   g. 1 heaping Tbls of finely diced red bell pepper
   h. Mix all ingredients together

2. Check 1 pound of precooked real crabmeat for shells and then gently blend the crabmeat in with the egg mixture

3. Lightly dampen hands and form 6 large or 12 small crab cakes (this can be done most easily by creating a ball, placing the ball on a plate covered with wax paper and then flattening the ball slightly)

4. Cover the crab cakes with more wax paper or plastic wrap and refrigerate for at least 2 hours. (If not refrigerated properly, the crab cakes will not hold together during sautéing.)

5. Take out of the refrigerator 15 minutes before cooking

6. Heat a large frying pan to medium high heat with 1 Tbls vegetable oil

7. Fry the crab cakes separated in the pan so they don't touch for 2 to 3 minutes per side, turning only once to help keep cakes from crumbling

Serve warm (no sauce is really necessary, but some people might want tartar sauce)

Grand Marnier Soufflé

I would suggest preparing the sauce first and keeping it warm in a double boiler until ready to serve

Sauce:

1. In a heavy sauce pan add:
    a. $\frac{2}{3}$ cup sugar
    b. $\frac{1}{3}$ cup Grand Marnier
    c. $\frac{1}{2}$ cup heavy cream
    d. 3 egg yolks (from large eggs)
2. Whisk until well blended
3. Add 8 Tbls (1 stick) unsalted butter cut into small pieces
4. Set over low heat and cook until thickened, stirring constantly (do not let boil)
5. Keep warm

Soufflé:

The soufflé can be made up to 1 hour in advance and covered until final baking

1. Preheat oven to 375 degrees Fahrenheit
2. Butter and sugar a 2-quart soufflé dish
3. Zest 1 orange
4. Separate 6 large eggs, placing 5 yolks in a large bowl (use the other yolk in the sauce)
5. Beat the 6 egg whites with a pinch of salt in another chilled bowl using an electric mixer (chill the beaters with the bowl before beating) until stiff but not dry, set aside
6. Melt 3 Tbls unsalted butter in a saucepan, add 2 Tbls flour, stir and cook for 1 minute over medium heat

NOTES

7. Remove from heat and add:
   a. 1 cup heavy cream
   b. $\frac{1}{3}$ cup sugar
   c. Zest from orange

8. Put back on heat and bring to a boil whisking constantly

9. Immediately remove from heat

10. Whisk the 5 egg yolks already in the large bowl until thickened

11. Slowly stir the warm cream mixture into the egg yolks

12. Add $\frac{1}{3}$ cup Grand Marnier and stir

13. Slowly add $\frac{1}{4}$ of the beaten egg whites and stir

14. Now, gently fold in the rest of the egg whites

15. Pour the mixture into the soufflé dish and smooth the top

16. Bake for 35 to 45 minutes until a skewer inserted into the center comes out clean

Serve immediately by spooning into small bowls and topping with orange sauce

Serving: Present the crudités first, arranged on a platter, with the drink of your choice. Plate a piece of quiche with a crab cake and serve. Make a really grand presentation by bringing the Grand Marnier Soufflé to the table in the soufflé dish. Put the sauce in a nice bowl. Spoon the soufflé into small individual bowls and top with the orange sauce with everyone watching and enjoy the "oohs and ahs."

Beverages

Champagne would be my first choice here but a White Bordeaux or dry Riesling would also pair well with this menu.

Coffee and fruit juice

Grandmother Wood Has a Change in Character

Edith and Henry Wood, Nan's grandparents, were the first in the family to own Sunny Shores cottage. They bought the little cottage in the early 1900s from a family on the north shore of the lake and then had to wait until winter when horses could slide the cottage across the frozen lake and put it on their lot where it sits today.

Mrs. Wood and Nan's mother, Mrs. Myers, were very proper ladies wearing hats and gloves to church, for example, so I always called them by their proper names only. They would look forward to my visits from my family cottage, "Orchard House", which was just down the lake. They loved pancakes so at least once each summer I would prepare the following menu. While waiting with some impatience, Mrs. Wood would begin rapping on the table with her knife handle to try and speed up the progress and Nan's mother would join in her loud chant, "We want pancakes, we want pancakes," both laughing at their wild behavior. My answer to this would be to serve Mrs. Wood one silver dollar size pancake on a very large plate with great flourish and announce that the balance would be served when I was good and ready. . . which was always immediately.

Both Mrs. Wood and Mrs. Myers were very grand ladies and two of the sweetest women I have ever known. We miss them both to this day.

Menu III

Grandmother Wood's Favorite Brunch
(6 Servings)

Sliced Fresh Peaches

Thick Sliced Bacon

Blueberry Pancakes

Scrambled Eggs with Smoked Salmon

This is a very simple menu that everyone will enjoy and can be expanded easily by doubling, tripling or even quadrupling the recipes. The only problem with increasing the recipe is the time to cook and keep the pancakes warm. Fresh peaches and blueberries appear late in the summer season in Michigan but are available from other sources earlier in the year and all year long in large cities.

Peaches

9 medium peaches

1 tsp sugar (or sugar substitute)

Bacon

1 pound thick sliced bacon

Blueberry Pancakes

$1\frac{1}{2}$ cups flour

$2\frac{1}{2}$ tsp baking powder

1 large egg

$1\frac{1}{4}$ cups whole milk

3 Tbls vegetable oil

1 pint blueberries

Salt

1 Tbls sugar

Pure maple syrup

1 pound unsalted butter (this will leave plenty for serving)

Scrambled Eggs

9 large eggs

$\frac{1}{4}$ cup cream (you can use half & half)

1 bunch chives

$\frac{1}{2}$ pound smoked salmon

$\frac{1}{4}$ tsp white pepper

$\frac{1}{2}$ tsp salt

1 Tbls unsalted butter

Sliced Peaches

This should be prepared at least 1 hour in advance but not overnight.

1. Peel 9 medium peaches, this is done most easily with a small paring knife. (Dipping the peaches in boiling water for a few seconds will loosen the skin and make peeling much easier.)

2. Slice the peaches into $\frac{1}{2}$ inch wedges, removing pits, and put in decorative bowl

3. Sprinkle with 1 tsp sugar (or sugar substitute) and $\frac{1}{4}$ cup cold water and stir (if peaches are not quite ripe you may need more sugar)

4. Cover the bowl and refrigerate until serving.

Bacon

1. Preheat oven to 350 degrees Fahrenheit

2. Use a good quality thick sliced bacon and prepare while the peaches are macerating (sitting in the simple syrup)

3. Using a large nonstick low sided cookie sheet, arrange bacon slices (usually 3 slices per person) with space between each piece

4. Bake for approximately 20 minutes until golden brown and crisp

5. Remove and put on paper towels to drain excess grease

Blueberry Pancakes

Of course you can use a packaged mix, but it is so easy to make your own.

Pancakes:

Makes about 1 dozen 5 inch pancakes

1. Mix together in a large bowl:
   a. $1\frac{1}{2}$ cups flour
   b. $2\frac{1}{2}$ tsp baking powder
   c. 1 Tbls sugar
   d. $\frac{3}{4}$ tsp salt
2. In another medium bowl mix together:
   a. 1 well beaten large egg
   b. $1\frac{1}{4}$ cups whole milk
   c. 3 Tbls vegetable oil
3. Pour the liquid mixture into the dry ingredients and stir until mixed but not smooth (do not beat until smooth or the pancakes will be tough; there should be some lumps)
4. Add 1 cup washed and dried fresh blueberries, mix slowly, again leaving lumps in batter
5. Let batter stand for at least 10 minutes before frying
6. Heat a pancake griddle or low sided nonstick fry pan to medium high heat
7. Spray or brush a very small amount of oil on pan and pour $\frac{1}{4}$ cup batter for each pancake
8. Turn pancakes only once when bubbles start to appear on top of batter
9. Keep warm in oven until all pancakes are cooked and ready to serve

Scrambled Eggs with Smoked Salmon

1. Separate 9 large eggs, putting the yolks and whites into separate bowls

2. Beat the whites until fluffy, but not stiff

3. Whisk the yolks until smooth and then:
   a. Add $\frac{1}{4}$ cup cream (or half & half) to the yolks and whisk until well mixed
   b. Add 1 Tbls diced chives and whisk
   c. Add $\frac{1}{2}$ tsp salt and $\frac{1}{4}$ tsp white pepper and whisk

4. Remove any skin and bones from $\frac{1}{2}$ pound smoked salmon

5. Flake into small pieces and add to the yolk mixture

6. Gently fold in the egg whites until whites disappear

7. Preheat a large nonstick skillet to medium high heat

8. Add and melt 1 Tbls unsalted butter

9. Pour in the egg mixture, stir and cook until desired doneness

Serving: Serve the sliced peaches in their decorative bowl with small bowls at each place. Serve the pancakes on a large warmed platter with the bacon around the edges. Serve unsalted butter and warmed pure maple syrup on the side. Serve any left over blueberries as another topper for the pancakes. Serve the scrambled eggs on a warmed platter with chopped chives on top as a garnish.

Beverages

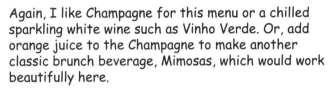

Again, I like Champagne for this menu or a chilled sparkling white wine such as Vinho Verde. Or, add orange juice to the Champagne to make another classic brunch beverage, Mimosas, which would work beautifully here.

Coffee and fruit juices

Honnie McClear Takes a Cooking Class

The Crystal Lake Art Center has been a growing and vital organization dedicated to promoting the arts since it was established in 1948. When I heard there were plans to expand the Art Center and move it into the old U.S. Coast Guard Station in Frankfort, I submitted a proposal for a Culinary Arts Program. Not only did the Art Center include the program in their plans, it wasn't long before I got the good news that someone had donated the money needed to refurbish the kitchen, and it would be named Kay's Kitchen in honor of the benefactor's mother.

Later, after one of my cooking classes, a student, Honnie McClear, approached me to say how much she had enjoyed the class especially since she got to sit in her mother's old kitchen. It turns out that Honnie's parents, John and Kay Nickum, were the original owners of Betsie Hosick's home where we are holding our cooking classes until the new Art Center is finished. Honnie told me what a great cook her mother had been. One of Honnie's fondest memories is of her mother preparing dinner in the kitchen and her father sneaking up behind her to kiss her on the cheek; and, yes, Honnie's mother is the Kay of Kay's Kitchen.

Honnie tells us that one of her mother's favorite soups was Vichyssoise with toast points.

Menu IV

Kay's Kitchen Brunch
(6 Servings)

Vichyssoise with Toast Points

Belgian Endive Salad

Baked Eggs in Tomato Boats

This is a very refreshing and light brunch with no meats. If you substituted vegetable broth for the chicken broth in the vichyssoise, it could be used as a vegetarian brunch. The vichyssoise can be prepared a day or two in advance and kept cold for last minute service, but make the toast points no more then an hour or two before serving so they don't become limp and soggy. The vinaigrette can also be made in advance and stored in the refrigerator, leaving last minute preparations to a minimum for an easy meal. If you would like to add something sweet to this menu, I would suggest sliced strawberries with heavy cream.

 *shopping List*

Vichyssoise

8 large leeks

3 Tbls unsalted butter

3 medium Yukon
gold potatoes

40 oz (5 cups) low sodium
chicken broth

1 cup heavy cream or
half & half

1 tsp fine salt

$\frac{1}{2}$ tsp white pepper

Bread of choice for toast points

(At least 12 slices of
bread for 6 servings)

Endive Salad

8 heads Belgian endive

4 large celery stalks

12 oz Stilton Blue Cheese
(you can use any Blue or
Roquefort cheese but I
prefer Stilton)

8 oz walnuts (whole, halves
or pieces)

1 bunch flat leaf parsley

Vinaigrette

4 Tbls red wine vinegar

2 tsp Dijon mustard

2 Tbls walnut oil

8 Tbls safflower oil

2 tsp fine salt

1 tsp fresh ground pepper

Tomato Boats

6 medium tomatoes

1 bunch fresh basil

6 large eggs

1 Tbls butter

Salt and pepper

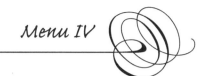

Vichyssoise

1. Clean and small chop the white part of 8 large leeks (save the green parts for stock)

2. Peel and thinly slice 3 medium Yukon gold potatoes

3. Bring a large soup pot to medium heat, add 3 Tbls unsalted butter

4. Add the chopped leeks and cook until tender, but not browned, about 5 minutes stirring occasionally

5. Add the sliced potatoes and 5 cups low sodium chicken broth

6. Bring to a boil, reduce heat to simmer and cook until potatoes are soft, about 30 minutes

7. Remove from heat and puree with an immersion blender or in a food processor until very smooth (if using a food processor, be very careful blending hot liquids; blend in small batches)

8. Season with 1 tsp fine salt and $\frac{1}{2}$ tsp white pepper

9. Add 1 cup heavy cream (you can use half & half, but not any other type of milk)

10. Store in refrigerator until ready to serve

Serve with toast points while the eggs are baking.

Toast points

Use bread of your choice

1. Cut crusts off bread and toast in toaster or oven to desired doneness

2. Cut on the diagonal for serving

Belgian Endive with Stilton, Celery, and Walnuts

Put the following in a large bowl:

1. Remove any discolored leaves from 8 heads of Belgian endive, cut in half, remove the hard core and slice thinly

2. Cut the heavy ends off 4 large celery stalks, use a vegetable peeler to de-string celery and slice thinly

3. Crumble 1½ cups Stilton cheese (you can use any blue or Roquefort cheese, but Stilton crumbles more easily and is not as creamy) and add to salad

4. Add 1 cup walnut pieces (you can use whole walnuts and chop to bite size pieces)

5. Add 1 bunch chopped flat leaf parsley (approximately 1 cup)

6. Mix together and chill until serving

Vinaigrette

1. Put the following in a blender, emulsify and chill until serving

    a. 4 Tbls red wine vinegar

    b. 2 tsp Dijon mustard

    c. 2 Tbls walnut oil

    d. 8 Tbls safflower oil

    e. 2 tsp fine salt

    f. 1 tsp freshly ground black pepper

Serving: Emulsify the vinaigrette again and pour over salad mix tossing lightly

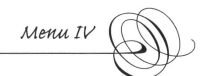

Baked Eggs in Tomato Boats with Herbs

1. Preheat oven to 350 degrees Fahrenheit

2. Wash and dry 6 medium tomatoes, cut a thin slice off the top (stem) side of tomato

3. Also slice a very, very thin slice off the bottom so tomatoes will stand up straight

4. Scoop out the contents of tomato with a small spoon (save for stock)

5. Turn tomatoes upside down on paper towels and let drain for at least 15 minutes

6. Put tomatoes in a buttered casserole dish

7. Sprinkle each lightly with salt and pepper and $\frac{1}{2}$ tsp chopped fresh basil

8. Break one large egg into each tomato and bake for about 30 minutes until egg whites are set

9. These should be served when done to avoid over cooking the eggs

Serve with the endive salad and more toast points

Serving: Serve the vichyssoise first in small bowls on a plate with the toast points. Emulsify the vinaigrette again and pour over salad mix, tossing lightly. Serve a tomato boat and some salad on individual plates with more toast points.

Beverages

Serve a white wine such as Pinot Gris or a non-oaky Chardonnay with this menu.

Coffee and fruit juice

Marjorie Prepares Her Own Brunch Party, Almost

Marjorie Elliott, one of my good friends and business partner, decided to have her own ladies' brunch party late last summer. Not known for her cooking abilities, I was a little surprised to hear she planned to prepare a fancy brunch for eighteen women. Marjorie is a good organizer and business woman but her idea of cooking is putting strawberries on top of Twinkies and calling it strawberry shortcake. I wondered how she was going to pull this off. I should have known. A week before the party, I got a call to make the spinach salad and the quiches and later found out that another good friend and cook, Kim Fairchild, got a call to make his liver pâté appetizer. She bought cookies and sorbet for dessert and even hired someone to help serve and clean up. The only thing Marjorie had to do was cook the maple bacon. . . she burned it so badly she couldn't serve it. That's our girl.

I worked with Marjorie to teach her the following menu, virtually doubling her repertoire.

Menu V

Easy Brunch Menu
(Serves 6)

Gazpacho Soup Sunny Shores

Eggs Florentine

Sausage Biscuits

Gazpacho is a light and fresh start to this menu. Eggs Florentine is a very old recipe that is almost a meal in itself. If you wish to make a vegetarian menu, just leave the sausage out of the biscuits. For a sweet addition to this menu, I would suggest an assortment of fudge or chocolate candies served with coffee after the meal.

Gazpacho Soup

1 medium English cucumber

1 medium green bell pepper

1 medium red onion

1 bunch flat leaf parsley

1 bunch chives

1 large egg (optional)

36 oz can petite diced tomatoes

8 oz V8 Vegetable Juice

$\frac{1}{4}$ cup red wine vinegar

3 Tbls extra virgin olive oil

2 garlic cloves

1 tsp salt

$\frac{1}{2}$ tsp pepper

Eggs Florentine

6 large eggs

12 oz small curd cottage cheese

12 oz Swiss cheese

6 oz Feta cheese

3 Tbls unsalted butter

1 10 oz package frozen chopped spinach

$\frac{1}{2}$ tsp nutmeg

Sausage biscuits

(makes about 18 small biscuits)

2 cups flour

1 Tbls baking powder

1 tsp salt

6 Tbls shortening (or unsalted butter)

1 cup whole milk

1 pound breakfast sausage

Butter and honey to serve with the biscuits

Gazpacho Soup Sunny Shores

NOTES

1. In a large bowl add:
   a. 1 medium English cucumber, peeled, seeded and finely diced
   b. 1 medium green bell pepper, cleaned and finely diced
   c. 1 36-oz can of petite diced tomatoes including juice
   d. $\frac{1}{2}$ cup V8 Vegetable Juice
   e. $\frac{1}{4}$ cup red wine vinegar
   f. 3 Tbls extra virgin olive oil
   g. 1 tsp salt
   h. $\frac{1}{2}$ tsp freshly ground black pepper

2. In a food processor puree and add to the bowl:
   a. 1 medium cleaned and quartered red onion
   b. $\frac{1}{3}$ packed cup flat parsley
   c. 2 minced garlic cloves
   d. 1 raw large egg (optional)
   e. $\frac{1}{2}$ cup V8 Vegetable Juice

3. Mix well and refrigerate for at least 2 hours (but not overnight, the flavor is much better if served very fresh)

4. Serve in chilled bowls with snipped chives on top along with the sausage biscuits

Eggs Florentine

This is so easy even "you know who can do it."

1. Take spinach from freezer and thaw in a strainer for at least 1 hour.

2. Preheat oven to 350 degrees Fahrenheit

3. Grease an 8 inch square baking pan (regular or nonstick will work)

4. In a large bowl whisk 6 large eggs

5. Add and mix:
   a. 12 oz small curd cottage cheese
   b. 12 oz grated Swiss cheese
   c. 6 oz crumbled Feta cheese
   d. 3 Tbls melted unsalted butter
   e. $\frac{1}{2}$ tsp nutmeg

6. Further drain the spinach by compressing it between your hands and then add to the bowl and mix

7. Pour the mixture into the greased pan and bake for about 1 hour, until a toothpick inserted in the center comes out clean.

8. Cool slightly and cut into serving pieces

Serve after the soup course with more biscuits

Sausage Biscuits

1. Preheat oven to 450 degrees Fahrenheit

2. Lightly fry 1 pound broken up breakfast sausage (do not overcook) and drain all fat through a strainer leaving a small amount of grease on meat

3. In a large bowl mix together:
   a. 2 cups flour
   b. 1 Tbls baking powder
   c. 1 tsp salt

4. Add 6 cut-up Tbls of chilled shortening (or unsalted butter) and blend in with a pastry blender or fork until mixture resembles coarse crumbs

5. Add 1 cup whole milk and blend with fork until thoroughly mixed

6. Mix in the drained sausage

7. Drop by heaping tablespoons onto an ungreased (nonstick is fine) cookie sheet about 1 inch apart

8. Bake for 12 to 15 minutes until golden brown

9. Keep warm until serving with butter and honey

Serving: Serve the gazpacho soup first in chilled bowls with snipped chives on top along with the sausage biscuits. Place butter and honey on the table for guests to top biscuits. Cut and serve the eggs Florentine on individual plates with more sausage biscuits.

Beverages

Serve Sauvignon Blanc with the gazpacho or, for the adventurous, a dry sherry such as Tio Pepe or La Ina. Switch to a light red wine, Valpolicella for example, with the eggs.

Coffee and fruit juice

NOTES

The Neighbors Next Door

David and Leslie are good friends and we are very lucky to have them as neighbors. They spend their winters in Texas and at one time Leslie had a cooking school in Austin that must have been very good, because she prepares some of the finest meals I have had the good fortune to share. Their kitchen windows open onto the space between our cottages, and periodically, well almost every night, we can hear David popping the cork as he opens wine for Leslie. Quite often we also see David advancing toward our garden with a pair of scissors to procure herbs for Leslie's latest delicacy. I first met David at a party at my old cottage, "Orchard House," when he was a teenager. Although I am a "few" years older than David, we like to get together and talk about old times at the Lake and contemplate the complexities of life while sitting out at the end of our dock around midnight.

We get to share many meals on the porch with David and Leslie during the summer and the following classic brunch is one of my picks to serve to them during the 2010 summer season.

Menu VI

Classic Brunch Menu
(Serves 6)

Caramel Pecan Brunch Cake

Classic Eggs Benedict

BBQ String Beans

Iced Lemon Cups

This is a true classic brunch menu which is not too hard to prepare and will bring raves from your family and guests. The brunch cake can be served hot or at room temperature and the dessert should be made the day ahead and put in the lemon cups just before serving. These are really elegant and a great end to a sumptuous meal. Don't be afraid of poaching the eggs and making the Hollandaise sauce, just follow the directions. It's really quite easy.

Brunch Cake and Topping

1 cup flour

1 Tbls baking powder

$\frac{1}{4}$ tsp salt

$\frac{1}{2}$ cup whole milk

5 Tbls unsalted butter

2 large eggs

1 cup sugar

2 tsp pure vanilla extract

$\frac{2}{3}$ cup brown sugar

4 Tbls cream

1 cup pecan pieces

Eggs Benedict

12 large eggs

1 Tbls white vinegar

1 tsp salt

6 English muffins

12 small thin slices cooked ham (your choice of type)

Hollandaise Sauce

$\frac{1}{2}$ cup unsalted butter (1 stick)

3 large eggs

1 large lemon (2 Tbls of fresh lemon juice)

$\frac{1}{4}$ tsp salt

1 pinch cayenne pepper

BBQ String Beans

2 pounds fresh green beans

4 slices smoked bacon

1 small yellow onion

$\frac{1}{2}$ cup ketchup

$\frac{1}{4}$ cup brown sugar

1 Tbls Worcestershire sauce

1 Tbls salt

Iced Lemon Cups

6 large lemons

1 envelope unflavored gelatin

1 cup sugar

Mint sprigs for garnish

Carmel Pecan Brunch Cake

1. Preheat oven to 350 degrees Fahrenheit

2. Grease a 9 inch square cake pan

3. In a small sauce pan over medium heat, add the following and heat thoroughly:

    a. $\frac{1}{2}$ cup whole milk

    b. $\frac{1}{2}$ Tbls unsalted butter

4. In a medium bowl:

    a. Whisk 2 large eggs until thick

    b. Add 1 cup sugar and 1 tsp vanilla and mix

5. In a large bowl add and mix:

    a. 1 cup flour

    b. 1 Tbls baking powder

    c. $\frac{1}{4}$ tsp salt

6. Slowly add the egg mixture to the dry ingredients and mix

7. Pour the hot milk mixture into the batter and mix quickly

8. Pour the batter into the cake pan and bake for about 25 minutes. A toothpick inserted into the middle of the cake should come out clean

See next page for the Brunch Cake Topping recipe.

NOTES

Cake Topping
(prepare while the cake is baking)

1. In a medium bowl add and cream together:
   a. 4 Tbls unsalted butter
   b. 4 Tbls cream
   c. $\frac{2}{3}$ cup brown sugar
   d. 1 tsp vanilla extract
2. Add 1 cup pecan pieces and mix
3. Spread over the top of the warm cake
4. Place under the broiler for about 1 minute to brown the topping
5. Serve hot, warm or at room temperature

BBQ Green Beans

NOTES

I would suggest preparing these before the eggs and keep warm until serving

1. Clean 2 pounds of fresh green beans

2. In a medium saucepan, bring 2 quarts of water to a boil with 1 Tbls salt

3. Add green beans and blanch until soft, approximately 3 to 4 minutes

4. Drain green beans and put in a large casserole dish

5. Preheat oven to 350 degrees Fahrenheit

6. Cut 4 slices of smoked bacon into $\frac{1}{2}$ inch pieces

7. Finely dice 1 small yellow onion

8. In a medium sauce pan fry the bacon and onion until the bacon is almost crisp and the onion is translucent

9. Add:
   a. $\frac{1}{2}$ cup ketchup
   b. $\frac{1}{4}$ cup brown sugar
   c. 1 Tbls Worcestershire sauce

10. Cook until sugar is dissolved

11. Pour on top of beans (do not stir)

12. Bake for about 20 minutes, keep warm until serving

Eggs Benedict

1. Take 12 large eggs and 12 small, thin slices of cooked ham from refrigerator before preparing to bring eggs and ham to room temperature (eggs need at least 2 hours but I prefer 4).

2. Break eggs into individual bowls, 4 at a time

3. Fill a large bowl with cold water and add 6 ice cubes

4. In a large frying pan place $1\frac{1}{2}$ inches of water, 1 Tbls white vinegar and 1 tsp salt

5. Bring to a soft boil (small bubbles on bottom of pan)

6. Add the 4 eggs, one at a time, and poach until whites are set. Do not try and move eggs until whites are set, about 3 minutes

7. Remove from pan with a slotted spoon, trim off any raggedy excess whites, and put in the bowl with the ice water

8. Repeat with 4 more eggs until all 12 are poached and in cold water

9. Split 6 English muffins and toast to desired doneness (keep warm)

10. In another large sauce pan heat 4 cups water to very warm, but not boiling

11. Next make the Hollandaise sauce:

    a. Melt $\frac{1}{2}$ cup (1 stick) unsalted butter, do not brown

    b. In an electric blender add:

        i. 3 egg yolks (discard the whites or save for another use)

        ii. 2 Tbls fresh lemon juice

        iii. $\frac{1}{4}$ tsp salt

        iv. 1 pinch cayenne pepper

    c. Turn on to low speed and while blending, add the melted butter slowly

    d. Blend about 15 seconds until sauce is thickened and smooth

12. Place 2 English muffins on each plate and top with ham slices

13. Carefully place the eggs from the cold water into the warm water for 1 minute

14. Remove eggs with slotted spoon, drain carefully and put one on each muffin

15. Spoon 2 Tbls of Hollandaise over each and serve immediately

NOTES

Iced Lemon Cups

NOTES

This recipe must be prepared one day in advance to allow time for duplicate freezing.

1. Clean 6 lemons and dry

2. Cut $\frac{1}{3}$ off the top of each lemon

3. Cut a very small slice off the bottom of each lemon so they will sit-up

4. Zest the peel from the top $\frac{1}{3}$ of each lemon, set the zest aside and discard the rest

5. Squeeze the juice from the bottom $\frac{2}{3}$ of each lemon, you need about $\frac{3}{4}$ cup (squeeze more lemons if necessary to get $\frac{3}{4}$ cup). Be very careful if using an electric juicer as it can collapse the lemon.

6. Remove the crushed insides of the 6 lemons and refrigerate the cups (do not freeze)

7. In a medium sauce pan over low heat add:
   a. $2\frac{1}{4}$ cups water
   b. 1 cup sugar
   c. 1 envelope unflavored gelatin

8. Cook until gelatin is dissolved, stirring constantly

9. Remove from heat and add the $\frac{3}{4}$ cup lemon juice and grated peel

10. Pour into a 9 inch square baking pan, cover with plastic wrap or foil

11. Put in freezer for about 3 hours until partially frozen

12. Spoon mixture into chilled large bowl and beat with electric mixer until smooth but still partially frozen

13. Return mixture to 9 inch pan, cover and freeze for 3 more hours until partially frozen (do not totally freeze)

14. Repeat beating again with electric mixer until smooth

15. Return mixture to pan, cover and freeze until firm (overnight)

16. Take mixture out of freezer 10 minutes before serving

17. Spoon into the lemon cups, top with a mint sprig and serve

Serving: Serve the brunch cake first with coffee or your special beverage. Plate 2 eggs Benedict with a small amount of the BBQ string beans for each person. Serve the balance of the beans in a bowl. Serve the lemon cups on individual plates garnished with extra mint.

Beverages

With all the flavors involved in this menu, it's tough to suggest a unifying wine. I would serve a chilled dry rosé such as Tavel from Provence but there are many fine dry rosés out there. The lemon cups need something sweeter such as a Muscat or white Port.

Coffee and fruit juice

Jim Makes Peking Duck for Fourteen

For the end of my second season of Dinner on the Porch Cooking Classes I wanted to do something really special and a bit showy. I decided to make one of my favorite dishes, Peking Duck. I had it for the first time when I was traveling in Hong Kong on business many years ago. That's where I learned that real Peking Duck, a national dish in China, consists of just the skin of a roasted duck served with Mandarin pancakes and green onions for brushing on the hoisin sauce. Delicious.

One of the challenges is that preparing Peking Duck requires you hang fresh ducks for several days before cooking. So where could I hang the six ducks I needed for class in this little cottage? I ended up hanging them from the cabinet doorknobs in our six-foot galley kitchen requiring that I keep very close watch over our two cats for the next three days. Several neighbors stopped by just to see the ducks including my good friend and the illustrator of my cookbooks, Chris Patterson. Chris decided she wanted to sketch the whole scene. The result is the beautiful drawing on this page.

You could easily substitute roasted duck meat for the chicken in Menu VII's salad – a perfect use for the duck meat after making Hong Kong Style Peking Duck.

Menu VII

Oriental Brunch Menu
(Serves 6)

Orange Marmalade Muffins

Warm Stir-Fry Chicken Salad

Oriental Fruit Bowl

Much of this menu can be prepared in advance if you serve the chicken salad cold. All the items for the chicken salad can also be prepared ahead and kept in the refrigerator until ready to stir-fry. I would suggest that the muffins would be best baked just before serving. The fruit bowl, except for the bananas and macadamia nuts, should be done the night before or at least 2 hours ahead so it can chill thoroughly and the flavors can blend. Peel and cut the bananas and add to the fruit bowl along with the macadamia nuts just before serving.

Muffins

$1\frac{1}{2}$ cups flour

$\frac{1}{2}$ cup sugar

1 tsp baking powder

1 tsp baking soda

1 tsp salt

$\frac{1}{2}$ cup orange juice

$\frac{1}{3}$ cup orange Marmalade

6 Tbls unsalted butter

1 large egg

$\frac{1}{2}$ cup golden raisins

More unsalted butter and orange marmalade for serving

Chicken Salad

1 head romaine lettuce

1 small head frisée or other delicate lettuce

1 bunch green onions

2 large carrots

3 whole (6 halves) boneless, skinless chicken breasts

8 oz pecan halves or pieces

2 Tbls chopped ginger

1 bunch fresh tarragon

$\frac{1}{2}$ cup soy sauce

2 Tbls sugar

2 Tbls olive oil

1 tsp sesame oil

Fruit Bowl

$\frac{1}{4}$ cup sugar

2 limes

1 14 oz can lychees in syrup (also known as lychee nuts)

1 ripe mango

2 Granny Smith apples or other tart apple

2 bananas

8 oz sliced macadamia nuts

Orange Marmalade Muffins
(makes 12 muffins)

NOTES

1. Preheat oven to 400 degrees Fahrenheit

2. Grease a 12-cup, nonstick muffin pan

3. In a small bowl mix the following together and set aside:

    a. $1\frac{1}{2}$ cups flour

    b. $\frac{1}{2}$ cup sugar

    c. 1 tsp baking powder

    d. 1 tsp baking soda

    e. 1 tsp salt

4. In a large bowl beat 1 large egg until frothy and add:

    a. $\frac{1}{2}$ cup orange juice

    b. $\frac{1}{3}$ cup orange marmalade

    c. 6 Tbls melted unsalted butter

5. Now slowly add the dry mixture and stir until just combined (do not try and beat to a smooth consistency)

6. Add $\frac{1}{2}$ cup golden raisins and stir lightly

7. Spoon the batter into the 12 muffin cups

8. Bake for 15 to 20 minutes

9. Remove and put muffins on wire rack to cool slightly before serving warm with unsalted butter and orange marmalade along with the warm chicken salad

NOTES

Warm Stir-Fry Chicken Salad

1. Put 3 whole (6 halves) skinless, boneless chicken breasts in the freezer for 20 minutes for easier slicing

2. Wash and dry 1 head of romaine and 1 small head of frisee (or other delicate lettuce) and keep cold until serving

3. In a small bowl add and mix:
   a. $\frac{1}{2}$ cup soy sauce
   b. 2 Tbls chopped ginger
   c. 3 Tbls finely chopped fresh tarragon
   d. 2 Tbls sugar

4. Take the chicken from the freezer and slice into thin strips across grain

5. Place chicken in a large bowl, pour the liquid mixture over and marinate for 1 to 2 hours in the refrigerator

6. While the chicken is marinating prepare the vegetables

7. Clean and cut 1 bunch of green onions into 1 inch pieces

8. Peel 2 large carrots and cut into fine strips using your peeler, making them about 2 inches long

9. Preheat a large wok or large deep sided frying pan on medium high heat and add:
   a. 2 Tbls olive oil and 1 tsp sesame oil
   b. Add the chicken strips and cook for 2 to 3 minutes
   c. Add the reserved marinade mixture and cook for another 2 to 3 minutes
   d. Add the green onions, carrots and 1 cup pecans (halves or pieces) and toss
   e. Immediately remove from heat

10. Place lettuce torn to small pieces on plates

11. Pile chicken mixture on top and serve

Oriental Fruit Bowl

1. In a small sauce pan add:

    a. The juice from one 14-oz can of lychees

    b. $\frac{1}{4}$ cup sugar

    c. $1\frac{1}{2}$ cups water

    d. The juice from 2 limes

2. Heat slowly until the sugar dissolves and then boil gently for 5 minutes

3. Remove from heat and let cool to room temperature

4. In a medium bowl put:

    a. The fruit from one 14-oz can of lychees

    b. 1 ripe, peeled, pitted and thinly sliced mango

    c. 2 peeled, pitted and thinly sliced apples
    (Granny Smith or other tart apple)

    d. Pour the liquid mixture over and chill for at least 2 hours

5. Add 2 peeled and thinly sliced bananas and 8 oz of sliced macadamia nuts and serve in small bowls

Serving: I would serve this entire menu at one time with the salad and a muffin on each plate and the fruit in small individual bowls.

Beverages

A less dry wine such as Gewurztraminer or a German Riesling would work well with this menu. The Gewurztraminer would pair especially well with the Oriental Fruit Bowl.

Tea, either hot or iced.

Bob and Betsie Host the 2009 Cooking Classes

Last winter, Betsie Hosick, one of my life-long Crystal Lake friends, very generously offered to host all of my 2009 Dinner on the Porch Cooking Classes in her lovely home overlooking Lake Michigan. I was delighted. It meant Betsie and her companion, Bob Weber, would be attending every class and I can't think of two people I would rather spend time with.

I doubled the number of classes from the previous year by doing one class in the morning and then repeating it in the afternoon. Bob and Betsie attended the morning session and then Betsie would generally leave during the afternoon. Bob, however, would sit on the sofa in the family room and nap during the afternoon session. I had a clear view of Bob, sound asleep, while I was teaching; that is until it was time to sample the prepared dishes. Bob, without fail, managed to wake-up just in time to be first in line. I can't really complain because Bob always adds a spark and bit of fun to the classes and, bless him; he washed most of the dishes after each class. He is a man of many talents.

Following is one of Bob and Betsie's favorite brunch menus. Bob particularly likes the French Toast.

Menu VIII

B & B Brunch
(Serves 6)

Coconut Granola with Yogurt

French Toast Crème Caramel

Mixed Fresh Fruit Bowl

This can be a totally prepare ahead menu that combines healthy yogurt along with a very tasty version of French Toast. If you like crème caramel you will love this recipe for French Toast. The toast and the granola must be prepared the night before, but the balance can be done just before serving. This is a completely vegetarian menu with no meat product included, although it does include eggs and milk. Ending the menu with a fresh fruit bowl will take the edge off the sweetness of the toast.

Granola

(This recipe makes enough granola for 20 $\frac{1}{2}$-cup servings)

5 cups old fashioned oats

$\frac{1}{2}$ cup wheat germ

$\frac{1}{2}$ cup sunflower seeds

$\frac{1}{2}$ cup walnut pieces

5 oz flaked coconut

$\frac{2}{3}$ cup honey

$\frac{2}{3}$ cup walnut oil

36 oz yogurt (plain or your choice of flavors)

French Toast

6 large eggs

2 cups whole milk

2 cups cream

$\frac{1}{3}$ cup sugar

1 tsp salt

1 loaf sliced cinnamon bread

1 Tbls pure vanilla extract

2 Tbls corn syrup

1 cup brown sugar

4 Tbls unsalted butter

8 oz sour cream (optional)

Fruit Bowl

I am listing fruits for this recipe, but you can and should choose and use fruits that are fresh and ripe at the time of preparation. The more citrus you use for this menu the more refreshing it will taste. For this recipe I would avoid fresh berries and bananas.

6 oranges

4 Ruby Red grapefruit

2 lemons

2 mangos

2 passion fruit

1 bunch cilantro

1 bottle dark rum (optional)

Granola with Yogurt
(makes approximately twenty $\frac{1}{2}$-cup portions)

1. Preheat oven to 350 degrees Fahrenheit

2. Prepare the granola 1 day to 1 week in advance and store in air tight container

3. In a large bowl combine and mix:
   a. 5 cups old fashioned oats
   b. $\frac{1}{2}$ cup wheat germ
   c. $\frac{1}{2}$ cup sunflower seeds
   d. $\frac{1}{2}$ cup walnut pieces
   e. 5 oz flaked coconut

4. Mix together $\frac{2}{3}$ cup honey and $\frac{2}{3}$ cup walnut oil and pour over the oat mixture

5. Spread mixture in a 9x12- inch, nonstick pan and bake for about 30 minutes or until golden brown, stirring every 10 minutes

6. Cool before serving

7. Serve about $\frac{1}{2}$ cup granola on top of 6 ounces of your favorite yogurt (for this menu I would use plain yogurt)

French Toast Crème Caramel

Be sure to prepare the night before, but no more than 24 hours in advance

1. In a medium sauce pan, melt over medium high heat until bubbly
   a. 2 Tbls corn syrup
   b. 4 Tbls unsalted butter
   c. 1 cup brown sugar

2. Pour mixture into a 11x17 inch glass baking pan (you can use a metal nonstick pan, but glass is preferred, due to its thickness)

3. Overlap 1 loaf of cinnamon bread slices by about $\frac{1}{2}$ of each piece in two rows on top of the syrup

4. In a large bowl:
   a. Whisk 6 large eggs until fluffy
   b. Add and mix well:
      i.   2 cups whole milk
      ii. 2 cups cream
      iii. $\frac{1}{3}$ cup sugar
      iv. 1 tsp salt
      v.   1 Tbls pure vanilla extract

5. Pour this mixture over the bread

6. Cover with foil and refrigerate overnight

7. Take from refrigerator about 2 hours before serving

8. Preheat oven to 350 degrees Fahrenheit

9. Bake covered for 40 minutes

10. Uncover and continue baking for another 10 minutes until puffed and golden brown

11. Cut into individual serving pieces

Serve with sour cream on the side (optional)

Fruit Bowl

Using a very sharp paring knife:

1. Peel and remove the skin and white pith from 6 oranges and 4 Ruby Red grapefruits

2. Using the same paring knife remove the wedges from between the membranes of the oranges and grapefruits and place in large bowl

3. Peel the skin from 2 mangos, cut the peeled fruit into pieces and put in bowl

4. Peel the skin from 2 passion fruits, cut the peeled fruit into pieces and put in bowl

5. Squeeze the juice from 2 lemons and put over fruit

6. Optional – Pour $\frac{1}{4}$ cup dark rum over top and stir (or serve rum at table)

7. Cover and refrigerate overnight or at least 2 hours

8. Serve in small bowls with garnish of cilantro leaves

Serving: The granola should be served first followed by the French toast and lastly the fruit. Plate the French toast individually with a dollop of sour cream. The fruit should be served in small individual bowls with a garnish of cilantro leaves.

Beverages

This menu seems to cry out for Mimosas but if you prefer serving wine, a German Riesling goes well with this menu or, if you can find it, an Argentine Torrontes.

Coffee

Jim Has His First Book Signing

Sally Berlin is the owner/manager of Crystal Crate and Cargo, a wonderful kitchen and gift store in Beulah, Michigan. Her store is a delight to anyone who likes to cook or entertain. Sally has been very helpful to me with my cooking classes, giving advice and lending support. When I told her my first cookbook, "Dinner on the Porch", would be published in May 2009, she very graciously said she would be happy to carry a few copies in the store. I really think she said she would do it more as a favor to me, not thinking that it would be something that would actually sell. So I had a box of cookbooks delivered to Crystal Crate and Cargo in early May. Sally called the day they were delivered saying how much she and her staff loved the book and wanted to have a book signing in the store during Memorial Day weekend. I was thrilled. They sold dozens of books at the book signing and throughout the summer. (It also helps that Kelly Luedtke, Kim Fairchild's sister, works in Crystal Crate and Cargo and likes to tell people about the book.) What a great start for my first cookbook.

As a celebration we had brunch the next day using the following menu.

Menu IX

Book Signing Menu
(Serves 6)

Savory Waffles with Seafood Sauce

Steamed Asparagus

Raspberries and Apples in Syrup

When most of us think of waffles, we think sweet and gooey with maple syrup and maybe fresh berries. This is a complete turn around and one worthy of the time and effort for the preparation. Don't let the list of ingredients overwhelm you, it is not that hard to prepare and oh the results. I would prepare this menu for a special brunch for friends that appreciate seafood and an elegant meal. It is possible to switch the seafood with left over roast turkey or chicken, but leave out the lemon juice. The asparagus, steamed in this case, rather than my usual roasted does not take any flavor away from the delicate seafood sauce. The raspberries and apples are a perfect finish served with shortbread cookies.

Waffles

2 cups flour

2 cups whole milk

2 large eggs

4 Tbls unsalted butter

1 Tbls baking powder

$\frac{1}{2}$ tsp Salt

1 bunch fresh chives

1 bunch fresh flat leaf parsley

1 bunch fresh thyme

Seafood Sauce

1 pound cooked crabmeat, lobster or shrimp (your choice or mix 2 or 3 together)

1 small yellow onion

1 bunch celery

4 Tbls flour

10 oz low sodium chicken broth

1 cup whole milk

6 Tbls unsalted butter

$\frac{1}{4}$ tsp salt

$\frac{1}{8}$ tsp pepper, white pepper preferred

2 fresh lemons

Asparagus

24 spears fresh asparagus

1 lemon

Salt

Raspberries and Apples

6 apples of your choice for poaching (I like Fuji apples for this recipe)

2 pints raspberries

$\frac{1}{2}$ cup sugar

6 black tea bags

1 lemon

Steamed Asparagus

1. Clean 24 spears of asparagus and cut into equal lengths
2. Put the following into a large covered frying pan:
   a. $\frac{1}{2}$ inch water
   b. 1 Tbls fresh lemon juice
   c. 1 tsp salt
3. Bring to a boil on high heat
4. Add the asparagus, cover and steam for 2 to 3 minutes
5. Remove immediately and keep warm until served

NOTES

Savory Waffles with Seafood Sauce

I would prepare the seafood sauce in advance and keep warm in a double boiler until ready to serve, but do not over cook or seafood will get tough. The asparagus will only take 3 or 4 minutes to steam so do them last.

Seafood Sauce:

1. Finely dice one small yellow onion

2. Finely dice 1 large stalk of celery

3. In a medium saucepan melt 6 Tbls unsalted butter over medium high heat

4. Add:
   a. $\frac{1}{3}$ cup diced onion
   b. $\frac{1}{3}$ cup diced celery
   c. $\frac{1}{4}$ tsp salt
   d. $\frac{1}{8}$ tsp fresh cracked pepper (white pepper preferred)

5. Sauté until onion is translucent, about 3 minutes

6. Add 4 Tbls flour and stir, let cook for 2 to 3 minutes

7. Add:
   a. 10 oz low sodium chicken broth
   b. 8 oz whole milk

8. Bring to a boil stirring constantly until thickened

9. Lower heat and add:
   a. $1\frac{1}{2}$ Tbls lemon juice
   b. 1 pound of cooked crabmeat (or your choice of seafood, which has been checked for any shells)

10. Transfer to a double boiler if not serving immediately and keep warm over low heat

Waffles:

This recipe will make 6 large or 12 small waffles

1. Preheat waffle iron
2. Preheat oven or warming drawer to 175 degrees Fahrenheit
3. Finely dice 1 Tbls fresh flat leaf parsley, set aside
4. Finely dice 1 Tbls fresh chives, set aside
5. Finely dice 1 tsp fresh thyme, set aside
6. Using 2 medium bowls, separate 2 large eggs
7. Beat the egg whites until fluffy (they do not need to be firm), set aside
8. In a large bowl add and mix:
   a. 2 cups flour
   b. 1 Tbls baking powder
   c. $\frac{1}{2}$ tsp salt
9. Whisk the 2 egg yolks and add:
   a. 2 cups whole milk
   b. 1 heaping Tbls fresh flat leaf parsley
   c. 1 heaping Tbls fresh chives
   d. 1 tsp fresh thyme
10. Whisk well to blend
11. Slowly add the liquid mixture to the dry mixture and mix (do not try to make a completely smooth batter)
12. Add 4 Tbls melted unsalted butter and stir until incorporated
13. Fold the fluffy egg whites gently into the batter
14. Let batter rest for about 10 minutes
15. Bake per directions of your waffle iron and keep warm until serving

Raspberries and Apples in Syrup

This should be prepared in advance or at least before any other part of this menu is started. You can serve this chilled, but it is best served at room temperature. Make the syrup first so that the apples will not turn brown.

1. Put 6 cups water into saucepan and bring to a boil

2. Add 6 black tea bags and steep for 5 minutes

3. Remove tea bags

4. Add $\frac{1}{2}$ cup sugar and 2 tsp fresh lemon juice

5. Peel, core and cut 6 apples (I like Fuji apples for this recipe) into bite size pieces

6. Add to the syrup and poach over medium heat for 5 minutes

7. Take off the heat and transfer to a large decorative bowl

8. Let cool to room temperature

9. Add 2 pints of raspberries, mix lightly and serve in individual bowls with a shortbread cookie

Serving: Place waffles on individual plates topped with about $\frac{1}{4}$ cup of the seafood sauce. Add a few asparagus spears on the side and serve.

Beverages

The beverage to serve with this menu is definitely a dry white wine, either a Pinot Blanc or Sauvignon Blanc.

Coffee

Cousin Jim Finally Writes Down His Chili Recipe

My cousin Barbara and her husband Jim Benjamin (known as Cousin Jim) are regular Sunny Shores visitors. Every year they come up from Cincinnati and Cousin Jim helps me get the cottage open for the summer and, most importantly, plants tomatoes and an herb garden. The other thing he does each year is make one or two batches of his famous chili. (Now I know that nearly everyone from Cincinnati claims to make a great chili but I can personally vouch for this one.) Jim lets his chili simmer for hours and hours, sometimes spanning a two day period, before declaring it ready to eat. On that night, we have one of the largest crowds in for dinner. People seem to somehow know it's chili night and aren't about to miss it. They bring their friends which is perfectly agreeable to Nan and me. Nan says friends are welcome, friends of friends are welcome, but draws the line at friends of friends' friends. It is a small cottage after all.

You're in for a real treat.

Cousin Jim's Chili Brunch
(Serves 8 generously with possibly some left-over chili)

Chili

Cornbread

Yogurt Sundae

This is cousin Jim's recipe that I had planned to put in "Dinner on the Porch", but Jim couldn't get it together in time for the printing. But here it is and it's perfect for a brunch on the porch, especially early or late in the summer season when the weather can be cooler or cold (it does happen in Michigan at times) and it might be raining. This is also a good day for a nice blaze in the fireplace. This was originally Jim's mother's recipe but Jim has zipped it up a bit over the years. A plain cornbread with lots of butter and a soothing yogurt sundae will smooth out the bite of the chili and finish out the meal perfectly. I also heavily recommend beer as the drink of choice, but some wine could also be served.

Chili

3 pounds 80% lean
ground beef

3 16-oz cans dark red
kidney beans

1 12-oz can diced tomatoes

1 16-oz can tomato sauce

1 6-oz can tomato paste

2 large onions

1 large green bell pepper

3 jalapeno peppers

1 head garlic

4 bottles of your
favorite beer

1 tsp seasoned salt

$\frac{1}{2}$ tsp garlic powder

$\frac{1}{2}$ tsp onion powder

3 Tbls A-1 steak sauce

1 Tbls soy sauce

2 Tbls apple cider vinegar

3 Tbls chili powder

$\frac{1}{4}$ tsp dried thyme

1 Tbls dried oregano

$\frac{1}{4}$ tsp dried basil

$\frac{1}{4}$ tsp black pepper

1 Tbls vegetable oil

Oyster crackers, chopped
onion, and cheddar cheese
to serve with the chili

Cornbread

$1\frac{3}{4}$ cups stone-ground
cornmeal

1 Tbls sugar

1 tsp baking powder

1 tsp baking soda

1 tsp salt

2 large eggs

1 pint buttermilk

Plenty of butter to serve
with the cornbread

Yogurt Sundae

1 quart plain yogurt

1 pint blueberries

1 pint raspberries

8 oz salted peanuts

3 Tbls brown sugar

Cornbread (Southern Style)
(Serves 8)

NOTES

Make the cornbread just before serving the chili so it is hot and moist, serve with lots of butter. You may want to double this recipe and make 2 skillets or pans, it will go fast.

1. Preheat oven to 450 degrees Fahrenheit

2. Grease a heavy 9 inch ovenproof skillet or an 8 inch square glass pan

3. In a large bowl add and mix together:
   a. $1\frac{3}{4}$ cups stone-ground cornmeal
   b. 1 Tbls sugar
   c. 1 tsp baking powder
   d. 1 tsp baking soda
   e. 1 tsp salt

4. In another bowl whisk 2 large eggs until frothy

5. Add 2 cups buttermilk and whisk

6. Add the wet ingredients to the dry ingredients and stir until just blended

7. Do not try to make a completely smooth batter

8. Pour into the skillet or pan

9. Bake for 20 to 25 minutes until top is browned and a toothpick inserted in the center comes out clean

10. Cut pieces and serve from skillet or pan to help keep cornbread warm with plenty of butter.

NOTES

Chili
(Serves 8)

Texans never put beans in their chili and this is somewhat of a compromise in that most of the beans are smashed helping to make the chili thicker. In Cincinnati, a favorite is to pour the chili over spaghetti and cover with finely chopped onions and your favorite cheese or with a hot dog on a bun. You can make the chili hotter by adding more jalapenos. The further ahead the chili is made, the better the flavor becomes.

1. Clean and finely chop 2 large onions

2. Clean and finely chop 1 large green bell pepper

3. Clean and dice 4 garlic cloves

4. Clean and finely dice 3 jalapenos, leaving seeds if you want hotter chili (Cousin Jim cuts a small piece off the end of the chilies and tastes for hotness then adjusts the recipe to only 2 jalapenos or up to 4 based on the heat)

5. In a large heavy bottomed pot, put 3 16-oz cans of drained dark red kidney beans and smash about 90% of the beans using a potato masher and put aside

6. In a large preheated skillet over medium high heat add 1 Tbls vegetable oil

7. Add 3 pounds of 80% lean ground beef and break- up as fine as possible

8. While browning add:

    a. 1 tsp seasoned salt

    b. $\frac{1}{2}$ tsp garlic powder

    c. $\frac{1}{2}$ tsp onion powder

9. When lightly browned (do not overcook) remove meat with slotted spoon and place in the pot with the smashed beans, leave all the oil in skillet

10. Add more oil if necessary and sauté the chopped onions, bell pepper, jalapenos, and garlic until onion is translucent, about 5 minutes

11. Put all this, including any oil into the bean pot

12. Add the following to the bean pot:

    a. 1 12-oz can of diced tomatoes with the juices

    b. 1 16-oz can of tomato sauce

    c. 1 6-oz can of tomato paste

    d. 3 Tbls A-1 Steak Sauce

    e. 1 Tbls soy sauce

    f. 2 Tbls apple cider vinegar

    g. 3 Tbls chili powder

    h. $\frac{1}{4}$ tsp dried thyme

    i. 1 Tbls dried oregano

    j. $\frac{1}{4}$ tsp dried basil

    k. $\frac{1}{4}$ tsp black pepper

    l. 3 bottles of beer (drink the 4th bottle yourself)

13. Stir well and simmer uncovered for at least 4 hours

14. If chili is too thick add water, if too thin continue cooking slowly

Serve in bowls with oyster crackers, chopped onions and shredded cheese placed on the table in separate serving bowls and, of course, the cornbread.

NOTES

Yogurt Sundae
(Serves 8)

This is the perfect ending to a somewhat hot and spicy meal and can be made a few hours ahead for ease in entertaining. I would not prepare it the night before but earlier in the morning is OK. You can use any berry or fruit of your choice.

1. Use a sundae glass or 8 oz tall drinking glass

2. Put 2 heaping Tbls of plain yogurt on the bottom

3. Put $\frac{1}{4}$ cup blueberries next

4. Put another 2 heaping Tbls of plain yogurt next

5. Put $\frac{1}{4}$ cup raspberries next

6. Add 1 heaping tsp brown sugar

7. Put 1 Tbls plain yogurt on top and add a few salted peanuts

Serving: Put the entire pot of chili and pan of cornbread on the table and serve family style. Make sure you have plenty of butter on the table. Put oyster crackers, chopped onions and shredded cheese in individual serving dishes so your guests can "dress" their own chili as they like. Serve the sundaes in their individual glasses after the chili course.

Beverages

Beer is the obvious choice here, but a South American Malbec is a good wine with chili if you have non-beer drinkers.

Jim Beck Lands at Every Cooking Class

Jim Beck is a retired Air Force Colonel who used to fly Bombers all over the world, executing precision landings in all kinds of weather. I only mention this because I think of it whenever I see him having to circle back two or three times to get his power boat into the lift that sits at the end of our dock on Crystal Lake. I suppose they are two very different things.

In all the years I've known Jim, I'd never known him to have an interest in cooking, so I was surprised when he signed-up for all of my Dinner on the Porch Cooking Classes. I assumed he was only coming to meet women and eat, not to learn how to cook. I was wrong . . . at least about learning how to cook. Recently, I've had several mutual friends tell me about the wonderful dinner parties they've been to at Jim's. They go on and on about the delicious coq au vin, crème brûlée, and chocolate mousse he's prepared, all of which are items from my cooking classes! Jim always invites me to his big July 3 cocktail party but maybe now I'll also get an invitation to dinner.

Menu XI is a menu I'm sure the Colonel will enjoy serving to his family and friends.

Menu XI

English Brunch
(Serves 6)

English Brunch Grill of Pork Chops, Lamb Chops and Sausages

Broiled Tomatoes

Ron's Potatoes

English Muffins with Jams

Orange Surprise

This is one of my favorite menus to serve and the meats and tomatoes can be cooked under the broiler or on the grill with the potatoes and oranges fixed in advance. I first had a brunch like this at the Brown's Hotel in London but it did not include the potatoes or oranges. They served baked eggs instead of the potatoes and the clotted cream and orange marmalade with scones instead of English muffins. It is one of my great memories of my first trip to Europe on business when I could afford to enjoy the more affluent things in life. It is a relatively inexpensive meal to prepare at home and really very easy.

Muffins

6 English muffins (get the real thing with lots of nooks and crannies)

1 jar clotted cream (usually available in the international section in a jar)

1 jar orange marmalade

1 jar strawberry jam

Unsalted butter

English Brunch Grill

6 thin pork chops
(not boneless)

6 rib lamb chops

12 link breakfast sausages

3 medium tomatoes

1 tsp dried oregano

1 tsp dried basil

1 tsp salt

$\frac{1}{2}$ tsp pepper

3 Tbls olive oil

Salt and pepper

Potatoes

8 medium Yukon Gold potatoes

1 medium yellow onion

1 stick unsalted butter

1 tsp salt

$\frac{1}{2}$ tsp pepper

Orange Surprise

6 medium navel oranges

2 Tbls sugar

$\frac{1}{2}$ tsp cinnamon

3 Tbls Triple Sec or Grand Marnier

30 seedless green grapes

Mint leaves for garnish

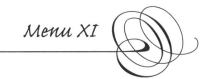

Orange Surprise

I would prepare the oranges first and allow them to marinate for 2 to 3 hours (but not overnight) and then prepare the potatoes which can be kept warm until serving.

1. Peel 6 medium navel oranges with a sharp paring knife, removing the peel and white pith.

2. Slice the oranges as thinly as possible crosswise and place in a large glass casserole dish

3. Sprinkle 2 Tbls sugar over the oranges

4. Sprinkle $\frac{1}{2}$ tsp cinnamon over oranges

5. Sprinkle 3 Tbls Triple Sec or Grand Marnier over oranges

6. Cover and refrigerate for at least 1 hour but preferably for 2 or 3 hours

7. Serve on individual plates with a few seedless green grapes and mint leaves for garnish

English Brunch Grill

NOTES

The pork, lamb, and tomatoes can be done at the same time under the broiler. The sausages should be prepared separately in a frying pan. This dish makes a wonderful brunch but can just as easily be served in the evening as an informal supper. It would be great to serve at a Monday night football party for example.

1. Prepare sausage:
   a. Preheat a medium size frying pan to medium high
   b. Add 1 Tbls olive oil to pan
   c. Fry 12 link breakfast sausages until lightly browned on all sides (do not over cook)
   d. Keep warm until serving

2. Preheat broiler

3. Prepare pork and lamb chops:
   a. Lightly brush each side of 6 thin, bone-in pork chops and 6 rib lamb chops with olive oil
   b. Sprinkle each side of both the pork and lamb chops using:
      i. 1 tsp salt
      ii. $\frac{1}{2}$ tsp freshly ground black pepper
      iii. 1 tsp dried oregano
   c. Put the pork and lamp chops on a low sided broiling pan with space so they don't touch
   d. Allow enough space to broil the tomatoes with the chops

Broiled Tomatoes

4. Prepare tomatoes:

    a. Cut 3 medium tomatoes in half crosswise

    b. Using a paring knife, make two slits diagonally across the cut side of the tomatoes

    c. Lightly brush cut side of tomatoes with olive oil

    d. Sprinkle each tomato using:

        i. 1 tsp salt

        ii. $\frac{1}{2}$ tsp freshly ground black pepper

        iii. 1 tsp dried basil

    e. Add tomatoes to broiling pan, cut side up, with the chops

5. Place pan under the broiler about 2 inches below fire or heating element

6. Grill for 2 minutes on first side

7. Turn over the chops (do not turn the tomatoes over if broiling tomatoes with the chops) and grill for another 1 minute

8. Remove and keep warm until serving

Ron's Potatoes

Ron Sarason is one of my best friends from Dallas, Texas and he always prepares these potatoes during my visits. Along with making the best spare ribs I've ever had, this recipe is tops.

1. Preheat oven to 400 degrees Fahrenheit

2. Peel and thinly slice 8 medium Yukon Gold potatoes and place in large bowl

3. Peel and finely chop 1 medium yellow onion and put in bowl with potatoes

4. Melt 1 stick unsalted butter and pour over potatoes and onions

5. Mix to coat and then sprinkle with 1 tsp salt and $\frac{1}{2}$ tsp fresh cracked pepper

6. Put into a large glass casserole and bake for about 1 hour turning occasionally

7. They should be crispy but not burned. Keep warm until serving

English Muffins

Toast the English Muffins until golden brown and keep warm

Serving: Place 1 pork chop, 1 lamb chop, 1 tomato and 2 sausages on each plate. Serve the potatoes in the casserole. Serve the muffins on the side with plenty of unsalted butter, clotted cream, orange marmalade and strawberry jam. The orange surprise makes a perfect ending.

Beverages

With the English Brunch Grill serve a medium-bodied red wine such as Rioja, Cotes-du-Rhone, or American red table wine.

With the Orange Surprise I recommend serving coffee and Cointreau.

And of course either hot tea or ice tea depending on your preference and the season.

About Laurel and Brad Heywood,
Sailboats, and Cookbooks

This wonderful couple helped me in many ways create and promote my first cookbook, "Dinner on the Porch." Brad, who spent several years in the publishing industry, gave me wonderful advice and counsel on getting it printed. And Laurel, bless her, gave a copy of the book as a hostess gift instead of the usual bottle of wine whenever they were invited to a dinner party last summer. Luckily for me, this popular couple gets invited to a lot of parties.

I met Laurel Hilton long before she married Brad. We used to race Wood Pussys (a small, very stable sailboat that our parents thought we couldn't tip over) at the Crystal Lake Yacht Club. We became good friends and I went to many parties at Laurel's family cottage, the "Crystal Hilton." Many cottages, whether very grand or very small, around the lake are named. No one needs an address, people say they are going to "such and such" for cocktails or dinner and everyone just knows where it is.

Brad and Laurel are in the process of transforming their cottage to a year around home with a cottage atmosphere. They have hosted many pot luck suppers over the years and I think the following large brunch menu would be perfect for brunch in their new home.

Note: I proved my parents wrong on more then one occasion – you can tip a Wood Pussy over.

Menu XII

Brunch for a Crowd
(12 servings – every recipe will serve 12)

Antipasto Platter

Eggplant Relish

Scotch Eggs

Brunch Cookies

This menu includes items that could be served for brunch or as appetizers for happy hour. It is set up to serve 12 but can easily be halved to serve 6 or expanded to serve an even larger crowd. I would serve a large basket of toasted breads of different types to go along with the antipasto and eggplant. This is a menu that you can prepare totally in advance and enjoy with your family and guests along with your favorite beverage. Nothing needs to be served warm.

Shopping List

Antipasto Platter

1 pound thinly sliced hard salami

1 pound thinly sliced Parma ham (you can use any smoked ham)

1 pound thinly sliced Monterey Jack cheese

1 pound thinly sliced Swiss cheese

1 pound baby Portabella mushrooms

1 package cherry tomatoes

1 can plain artichoke hearts

1 can pitted black olives

1 jar roasted red peppers

1 cup white wine vinegar

$\frac{3}{4}$ cup extra virgin olive oil

1 medium yellow onion

5 large cloves garlic

2 tsp sugar

1 bunch fresh basil

1 bunch fresh oregano

1 tsp freshly ground black pepper

1 loaf thinly sliced sour dough bread

1 thinly sliced baguette French bread

1 jar Dijon mustard

1 bunch red leaf lettuce for decorating

Eggplant Relish

2 large eggplants

1 large yellow onion

2 large red bell peppers

3 large ripe tomatoes

2 lemons

3 Tbls extra virgin olive oil

$1\frac{1}{2}$ tsp Salt

$\frac{3}{4}$ tsp pepper

Scotch Eggs

16 large eggs

$1\frac{1}{2}$ pounds sage sausage

2 cups bread crumbs

4 Tbls flour

Salt and pepper

2 cups vegetable oil for deep frying

1 cup good mayonnaise

1 jar Dijon mustard for serving

Brunch Cookies

1 cup dried apricots

1 cup corn flakes

1 cup oatmeal

1 cup flaked coconut

2 cups flour

$\frac{1}{2}$ tsp baking powder

$\frac{1}{2}$ tsp baking soda

$\frac{1}{2}$ tsp salt

$\frac{3}{4}$ cup shortening

$\frac{3}{4}$ cup brown sugar

$\frac{3}{4}$ cup sugar

2 large eggs

1 tsp pure vanilla extract

Eggplant Relish (sometimes called Poor Man's Caviar)

NOTES

1. Preheat oven to 425 degrees Fahrenheit

2. Pierce 2 large eggplants with a fork and bake on a cookie sheet for 20 minutes

3. Eggplant should be soft but not collapsed

4. Let eggplant cool until easy to handle then cut in half lengthwise

5. Scoop out and chop the eggplant meat coarsely and put in large bowl

6. Add and mix well:

   a. 1 large yellow onion finely chopped

   b. 2 large red bell peppers finely chopped

   c. 3 large ripe tomatoes finely chopped (drain excess juice)

   d. 3 Tbls extra virgin olive oil

   e. The juice from 2 lemons

   f. $1\frac{1}{2}$ tsp salt

   g. $\frac{3}{4}$ tsp fresh ground black pepper

7. Refrigerate for at least 2 hours or overnight

Serve in bowl with small spoon

Antipasto Platter

NOTES

Prepare everything at your leisure, but arrange the antipasto platter last.

1. In a large shallow pan place:
   a. 1 pound cleaned baby Portabella mushrooms
   b. 1 package cherry tomatoes
   c. 1 can plain artichoke hearts, drained
   d. 1 can pitted black olives, drained
   e. 1 jar roasted red peppers, drained
2. Peel and dice 1 medium yellow onion
3. Peel and dice 5 large garlic cloves
4. Finely chop 2 Tbls each of fresh basil and oregano
5. In a medium saucepan add:
   a. 1 cup white wine vinegar
   b. $\frac{3}{4}$ cup extra virgin olive oil
   c. The diced onion
   d. The diced garlic
   e. The 2 Tbls each of basil and oregano
   f. 2 tsp sugar
   g. 1 tsp freshly ground black pepper
6. Bring this to a boil, reduce heat and simmer for 5 minutes
7. Let cool to room temperature and pour over the vegetables in the pan
8. Mix to coat all vegetables
9. Cover and refrigerate for 12 hours or overnight
10. Drain vegetables well and bring to room temperature
11. Clean and arrange red leaf lettuce on large platter

12. Arrange vegetables around platter with 1 pound thinly sliced hard salami, 1 pound thinly sliced Parma ham (you can use any smoked ham), 1 pound thinly sliced Monterey jack cheese, and 1 pound thinly sliced Swiss cheese.

13. Thinly slice and toast 1 loaf of sourdough bread and 1 French bread baguette

Serving: Put the toasted bread in large basket lined with a napkin. Put Dijon mustard in a bowl with a small serving spoon to serve with the antipasto and eggs. Place the bread basket and Dijon mustard on a buffet along with the antipasto platter.

Scotch Eggs

NOTES

These are very popular and will generate lots of questions about how you prepared them with the egg in the middle. You may want to make more as they are still good the next day.

1. Bring 16 large eggs to room temperature by removing the eggs from the refrigerator for at least 2 hours but preferably 4

2. Hard boil 12 eggs as follows:
   a. Place in a pan one layer deep with room so they are not crowded, cover completely with water
   b. Bring to a light boil, remove from heat, cover pan and let stand for 15 minutes
   c. Drain hot water, place pan in sink and run cold water over eggs until they are at room temperature or just warm to touch

3. Immediately crack eggs and remove shell (If not using until later put in bowl, cover and refrigerate but bring back to room temperature before continuing)

4. Bring $1\frac{1}{2}$ lbs of sage sausage to room temperature

5. On a piece of wax paper, divide the sausage into 12 balls

6. Flatten each ball in a circle big enough to cover an entire egg

7. In a medium bowl combine:
   a. 2 cups bread crumbs
   b. 1 tsp salt
   c. $\frac{1}{2}$ tsp black pepper

8. In another medium bowl whisk the other 4 raw eggs until lightly beaten

9. In another bowl put 4 Tbls of flour

10. Roll each egg in the flour to coat entirely

11. Place egg in center of sausage circle and press sausage around, covering the egg completely

12. Dip the sausage covered egg into the beaten eggs

13. Roll the egg in the bread crumbs to coat on all sides

14. Finish coating all eggs before deep frying

15. Using a deep fryer or high sided pan, heat enough oil to cover eggs to 360 degrees

16. Fry eggs until golden brown, about 2 to 3 minutes, do 3 to 4 eggs at a time

17. Drain on paper towels

Serving: Refrigerate if not serving until the next day but return to room temperature before serving. Cut the eggs in half and serve with Dijon mustard and mayonnaise. (If desired, you can serve the eggs warm if you do it right after deep frying.)

NOTES

Brunch Cookies
(Serves 12)

1. Preheat oven to 375 degrees Fahrenheit

2. Lightly grease a large cookie sheet

3. In a large bowl combine and mix:
   a. 1 cup diced dried apricots
   b. 1 cup corn flakes
   c. 1 cup oatmeal
   d. 1 cup flaked coconut
   e. 2 cups flour
   f. $\frac{1}{2}$ tsp baking powder
   g. $\frac{1}{2}$ tsp baking soda
   h. $\frac{1}{2}$ tsp salt

4. In another large bowl combine and mix:
   a. 2 large beaten eggs
   b. 1 tsp pure vanilla extract
   c. $\frac{3}{4}$ cup shortening
   d. $\frac{3}{4}$ cup brown sugar
   e. $\frac{3}{4}$ cup sugar

5. Add the dry ingredients slowly to the wet ingredients, stirring until a firm dough forms, do not over mix

6. Divide the dough into 12 large or 24 small balls

7. Flatten the balls on the cookie sheet

8. Bake for approximately 15 minutes until golden brown

Cool to room temperature and serve

Serving: Serve all items as a buffet on decorated platters with plates and cloth napkins – no eating utensils are needed.

Beverages

This menu calls out for an Italian wine of course. A light Italian red Sangiovese such as a Chianti, a Valpolicella, or a Veneto all work well here. A nice selection of bottled beers would also go well with this menu.

Charlie Fairchild's Christmas Sausage Now Available

Kim Fairchild is one of my closest friends. He is one of the lucky people who live in Frankfort year-round, one of the "Townies" as we used to say when I was a kid. (Summer people who spent more then two weeks in the area were called "Lakies" and people renting for two weeks or less were called "Fudgies" because of all the local fudge they bought.) Kim is a great cook and has been the inspiration for many dinner parties and recipes in my cookbooks. His interest in food began at a very young age. Kim's grandfather, Charlie Fairchild, owned a market in town that had the best meat in the area. All of our mothers used to shop there. One of the items Charlie was famous for was his Christmas Sausage. It was so popular that after the Fairchild Market closed, the local IGA started making it and would hang a big banner in the window saying "CHARLIE FAIRCHILD'S CHRISTMAS SAUSAGE NOW AVAILABLE." Kim and his sister Kelly graciously provided me with Charlie's recipe and I've included it here.

Additional Brunch Selections

Charlie Fairchild's Christmas Sausage

Cottage Cheese Pancakes

Potato Pancakes

Brunch Egg Casserole

Lobster Pot Pie

Ham Soufflé

Grilled Asian Salmon

Triple Chocolate Gelato

NOTES

Charlie Fairchild's Christmas Sausage
(24 to 30 patties)

This recipe originally came from Kim Fairchild's grandfather who made it every year to sell in the old Fairchild Market at Christmas. Kelly Luedtke, Kim's sister, gave this recipe to everyone in one of my cooking classes in the summer of 2009. Originally it was to be made in large quantities starting with 25 pounds of pork and put into pork intestines to make long links which were coiled to form a large round shape held together with a long skewer for presentation. I have reduced the recipe to one quarter the size and suggest making patties rather than stuffing casings.

Shopping List

6 pounds ground pork shoulder

3 Tbls salt

$\frac{1}{2}$ bunch finely chopped flat leaf parsley

$\frac{1}{4}$ pound finely chopped pecans

1 Tbls nutmeg

$\frac{1}{2}$ Tbls white pepper

$\frac{1}{2}$ cup heavy cream

Preparation

1. Put all ingredients into a food processer and pulse to mix thoroughly (do not over mix). You may have to do this in batches depending on the size of your food processer.

2. Dampen your hands and form into patties the size of your choice

3. Refrigerate until usage

4. Fry patties in skillet over medium heat until lightly browned on both sides and firm, about 5 minutes on each side depending on the thickness of the patties. Do not overcook.

Serve with your choice of eggs or maybe The English Grill Brunch instead of the links included in the menu.

Cottage Cheese Pancakes

(Serves 4)

This could be a possible lower calorie and carbohydrate replacement for the blueberry pancakes in Grandmother Wood's brunch. This recipe serves four, due to the fact that you will need a blender and most household blenders are not large enough to accommodate a bigger recipe. Just make two batches before frying for larger groups of family and friends. This recipe is the courtesy of Jeri Richardson.

Shopping List

6 large eggs – separated

$\frac{1}{2}$ tsp salt

2 tsp pure vanilla extract

2 cups cottage cheese (not low fat)

$\frac{1}{2}$ cup flour

Preparation

1. Put the egg whites in the blender and whip until very frothy

2. Add the egg yolks, salt and vanilla and whip again

3. Add the cottage cheese and whip until smooth

4. Add the flour and whip until smooth. The batter will be quite thin, it's okay

5. Fry as you would any pancake and serve with butter and heated maple syrup and/or fresh berries.

Potato Pancakes
(Serves 6)

This recipe could be substituted for the Savory Waffles if you don't have a waffle iron or want to create a more substantial meal. You could also serve these pancakes with sour cream and homemade applesauce along with bacon or the Christmas Sausage for a complete brunch.

Shopping List

4 large potatoes

1 medium yellow onion

2 large eggs

5 Tbls flour

2 tsp salt

$\frac{1}{4}$ tsp freshly ground black pepper

Vegetable oil for frying

Preparation

1. In a large bowl beat the eggs until smooth

2. Add the flour, salt and pepper and mix

3. Peel the potatoes and shred with a coarse grater, add to the bowl with the egg mixture

4. Peel the onion, shred and add to the potato mixture

5. Mix well

6. Using a large nonstick skillet on medium high heat add a small amount of oil to just cover bottom of pan

7. Drop potato mixture by heaping $\frac{1}{4}$ cup amounts into pan and flatten with a spatula

8. Fry until golden brown, about 4 minutes and turn to brown other side

9. Keep warm in preheated 200 degree Fahrenheit oven until ready to serve

Brunch Egg Casserole
(Serves 6)

This recipe is fast and easy and is prepared the night before to be baked the next day. Serve with some fresh fruit and muffins for a complete meal.

Shopping List

10 large eggs

$2\frac{1}{2}$ cups whole milk

1 tsp salt

$\frac{1}{2}$ tsp freshly ground black pepper

1 tsp dry mustard

1 cup extra sharp Cheddar cheese

1 pound cooked broken up sage pork sausage
(you can use turkey sausage)

8 slices thick sliced bread (okay to leave crusts on) cut into about 1 inch cubes

Preparation

1. Butter a 9x13 inch baking pan (preferably glass)

2. In a large bowl beat the eggs with an electric mixer or whisk until very smooth

3. Add the whole milk, salt, pepper and mustard and mix well

4. Stir in the bread cubes, cheese and sausage, mixing thoroughly

5. Spread the mixture into the prepared casserole, cover with foil and refrigerate overnight, but at least 12 hours

6. Take out of refrigerator and remove foil 1 hour before baking

7. Preheat oven to 350 degrees Fahrenheit

8. Bake for 35 to 40 minutes

9. Let cool for 10 minutes and cut into squares for serving

Lobster Pot Pie
(Serves 4)

This is one of my latest and now one of my very best and favorite recipes. It makes a great presentation and served along with a delicate salad with a light vinaigrette, makes an elegant brunch menu. You can substitute shrimp, left over from a cocktail party, or crab meat for the lobster. You will need four 10-oz to 12-oz bowls

Shopping List

1 large yellow onion

1 large fennel bulb

1 stick unsalted butter

$\frac{1}{2}$ cup flour

$2\frac{1}{2}$ cups clam juice

1 Tbls Sambuca

1 Tbls salt

$\frac{3}{4}$ tsp white pepper

4 Tbls heavy cream

1 pound cooked lobster meat

1 cup frozen peas (thaw at room temperature in strainer for at least 1 hour)

1 cup frozen pearl onions (thaw at room temperature for at least 1 hour on paper towels)

1 cup baby portabella mushrooms cut into bite size pieces

1 bunch flat leaf parsley

1 large egg

Enough pastry dough to cover the tops of the bowls (either fresh or frozen)

Preparation

1. Preheat oven to 350 degrees Fahrenheit
2. Peel and finely dice the onion
3. Clean and finely dice the fennel
4. In a large sauté pan over medium heat melt the stick of unsalted butter
5. Add the diced onion and fennel
6. Sauté for about 10 minutes until the onions are translucent
7. Add $\frac{1}{2}$ cup flour and sauté over medium low heat for 3 minutes, stirring frequently
8. Slowly add:
   a. $2\frac{1}{2}$ cups clam juice
   b. 1 Tbls Sambuca
   c. 1 Tbls salt
   d. $\frac{3}{4}$ tsp white pepper
9. Simmer for 5 minutes and add the 4 Tbls heavy cream
10. Cut the lobster meat into bite size pieces and add to pan
11. Add 1 cup pearl onions, 1 cup peas, and 1 cup portabella mushrooms to pan
12. Dice $\frac{1}{2}$ cup parsley and add to pan
13. Lightly mix and check seasonings
14. Divide the mixture evenly between the 4 bowls
15. Cut rounds of the pastry dough large enough to overlap the bowls
16. Make an egg wash with 1 large egg and 1 tsp water
17. Lightly brush the top edge of the bowls with the egg wash
18. Place dough rounds on bowls and press against sides of top edge
19. Brush tops of dough covered bowls with the egg wash
20. Make 2 to 3 slashes in dough crust to release steam
21. Bake for 1 hour or longer until crust is golden brown and filling is bubbling

Serve with a salad and wine for a complete meal

Ham Soufflé

(Serves 6)

This recipe can be prepared in a 6 cup soufflé dish or individually in 8-oz dishes. I especially like this served in individual soufflé dishes. Again, this could be a complete menu served with fresh fruit and muffins or toast. I would make a fruit salad from local ripe fruit with a touch of rum and serve with fresh warm croissants.

Shopping List

6 large eggs

$\frac{3}{4}$ cup cream or whole milk

$\frac{1}{2}$ tsp dry mustard

$\frac{1}{4}$ tsp white pepper

$1\frac{1}{4}$ cup shredded white Cheddar cheese

8-oz room temperature cream cheese cut into small pieces (this is more easily done by cutting while cold and then left to warm on a plate)

$1\frac{1}{2}$ cups finely diced cooked ham

1 tsp finely diced flat parsley

Preparation

1. Preheat oven to 375 degrees Fahrenheit
2. Using a food processor add:
   a. The eggs, cream, mustard and pepper
   b. Cover and blend until smooth
   c. Add the Cheddar and cream cheese
   d. Cover and pulse until smooth
3. Stir in the ham and parsley
4. Pour into individual or large dish and bake for 25 to 30 minutes until set

This is best served warm.

Grilled Asian Salmon
(Serves 4)

This can be prepared on an outdoor grill, but is best done on an indoor grill as it only takes a few minutes to cook and the marinade could flame with hot coals. The marinade enhances, but does not take away the delicate flavor of the salmon.

Serve with a light salad and warm rolls for a quick easy brunch.

Shopping List

$1\frac{1}{2}$ pound wild-caught salmon filet (approx 6 oz per person)

6 Tbls extra virgin olive oil

4 Tbls soy sauce

2 Tbls Dijon mustard

$\frac{1}{2}$ tsp minced garlic

Preparation

1. Cut salmon filet into 4 pieces and place flat in glass casserole dish

2. Make marinade:

   a. Put the olive oil, soy sauce, mustard and garlic in small bowl and mix well

   b. Pour the marinade over salmon filets, cover with plastic wrap and marinate for 2 to 3 hours in refrigerator

3. Preheat grill on high heat until it lightly smokes

4. Grill salmon filets skin side down first, without wiping off marinade, for 2 to 3 minutes

5. Turn filets over and grill for another 2 to 3 minutes (do not overcook)

6. Heat the balance of the marinade in small sauce pan, pour over salmon and serve

Triple Chocolate Gelato
(Serves 4)

This is a wonderful and very special dessert that fits with almost any brunch, lunch, or dinner.

You will need an ice cream maker.

Shopping List

2 cups whole milk

$\frac{1}{2}$ cup heavy cream

$\frac{3}{4}$ cup sugar

1 cup unsweetened cocoa powder

2 oz bittersweet chocolate, chopped

4 large egg yolks

2 Tbls Kahlua

2 tsp pure vanilla extract

1 pinch salt

4 oz milk chocolate (with nuts and nugget if desired), chopped

Preparation

1. In a large sauce pan add:
    a. 2 cups whole milk
    b. $\frac{1}{2}$ cup heavy cream
    c. $\frac{1}{2}$ cup sugar
2. Heat until sugar dissolves and milk starts to simmer (do not boil)
3. Add and whisk until smooth:
    a. 1 cup unsweetened chocolate powder
    b. 2 oz. chopped bittersweet chocolate
4. Set aside

5. Using an electric mixer with large bowl add:
   a. 4 large egg yolks
   b. $\frac{1}{4}$ cup sugar

6. Beat on high speed for 3 minutes until yolks are very thick

7. With the mixer on low speed, slowly pour in the chocolate mixture and blend

8. Pour the egg and chocolate mixture back into the sauce pan

9. Cook over medium low heat until thickened, stirring constantly (do not boil)

10. Pour the mixture thru a sieve into another bowl, add and stir:
    a. 2 Tbls Kahlua
    b. 2 tsp pure vanilla extract
    c. 1 pinch salt

11. Place a piece of plastic wrap directly on top the mixture and chill completely

12. Pour the custard into the bowl of an ice cream maker and process according to manufacturer's directions

13. Stir in the roughly chopped milk chocolate and freeze in covered container

14. Allow the Gelato to lightly thaw before serving

NOTES

Larry Lars Gets the Girl but not the Pie Crust Recipe

Larry "Lars" Hilton is one of my good friends and has been coming to dinner and brunch on the porch for several years. Last summer Lars brought a guest to one of our brunches, a lovely woman named Beth Tabbert, and it came to light that he and Beth had been dating for several months over the winter. For her first meal at Sunny Shores, Beth brought wonderful lime tarts for everyone to have for dessert. It turns out that Beth is a terrific baker, something she has in common with Lars. In fact, her pie crust is one of the best I've ever had but when I asked her for the recipe, she refused to give it to me! The recipe is an old and well guarded secret handed down to the women in her family. Even Lars has tried to get it out of her with no success. Beth and Lars have been happily together for almost two years now and still no recipe. Looks like Larry Lars got the girl but not the pie crust recipe.

Additional Beverage Suggestions

Coffee

Blackberry Ice Tea

Petoskey Peach Cooler

Bloody Mary

Sarasota Rum Peach Sunrise

Charged Iced Coffee

Coffee of course is a must for most brunches. Almost everyone has his or her own favorite way of preparing it and I've included mine here. The other beverages included here are great brunch drinks and will liven up any party when you want something besides coffee, wine, or fruit juices. These drinks, along with the Wine, Champagne and Beer suggestions should give you some good choices for your "Brunch on the Porch"

Coffee

NOTES

I know everyone has his or her own favorite way of preparing coffee. I'll share mine with you here. I use a standard drip coffee maker with the following: dark roast coffee beans which I grind just before brewing, cold fresh water and a pinch of salt. I do not brew until just before serving and do not let the pot sit on high heat to keep warm. I put it in a coffee thermos to keep warm. Leaving the pot on heat reduces the coffee, just like reducing a sauce to get more intensified flavor, and gives the coffee a more bitter taste.

Blackberry Ice Tea
(Serves 6)

Ice tea is another brunch staple, especially in the summer. This is a little fancier version of basic ice tea and makes the drink special. Your guests will love it.

Shopping List

6 blackberry tea bags

$\frac{1}{4}$ cup orange juice

Lemons

Fresh mint

Preparation

1. In a large, heat-proof pitcher, place 6 blackberry tea bags

2. Bring 12 cups of water to a boil and pour over the tea bags

3. Leave the pitcher on the counter with the tea bags in the water until the whole thing cools to room temperature, at least an hour

4. Remove tea bags

5. Add $\frac{1}{4}$ cup orange juice and several lemon slices

6. Cover and chill until ready to serve

7. Serve in tall glasses with lots of ice, a slice of lemon and a mint leaf.

NOTES

115

Petoskey Peach Cooler
(Serves 6)

Petoskey is one of my favorite cities in Michigan and you can get wonderful fresh peaches there during the summer. I would suggest doubling the recipe as it will go fast.

Shopping List

2 peaches

1 bottle Sauvignon Blanc

1 bunch fresh mint

Preparation

1. Bring a medium sauce pan of water to a boil

2. Put the 2 peaches in the water for a few seconds for easier peeling

3. Put the 2 peeled peaches in a large pitcher

4. Add 6 mint leaves

5. Add the bottle of wine

6. Let steep for at least 4 hours

7. Serve over ice with a mint leaf and a slice of the peach from the pitcher.

Bloody Mary
(Serves 1)

This is my favorite Bloody Mary recipe. The Cove restaurant in Leland Michigan adds a smoked chub to their drink instead of celery and calls it a "Chubby Mary." Try it if you like smoked fish, it's a great conversation piece. Serve with a knife and fork and crackers on the side.

Shopping List

$1\frac{1}{2}$ oz vodka (I like Absolut or Blue Ice)

4 oz V8 Juice

1 tsp fresh lemon juice

$\frac{1}{4}$ tsp celery salt

$\frac{1}{4}$ tsp freshly ground black pepper

1 dash Worcestershire

Preparation

1. Put all ingredients in a shaker with ice and shake until well blended.

2. Pour into a tall glass with ice and add your choice of either:
   a. 1 stick of celery
   b. 1 smoked chub
   c. 1 long wedge cucumber
   d. 1 green onion

Sarasota Rum Peach Sunrise

(Serves 6)

I spend most of the winter in Sarasota, Florida but remember a drink I had as a child in California called an "Orange Julius". This is my adult version of that drink.

Shopping List

1 large peach

4 cups fresh orange juice

$\frac{1}{2}$ cup whole milk

$\frac{1}{2}$ cup white rum

$\frac{1}{4}$ tsp pure vanilla extract

Preparation

1. Peel, seed and cut the peach into small chunks

2. Put all of the above ingredients into a blender and mix until smooth

3. Pour over ice and serve

Charged Ice Coffee
(Serves 6)

For something a little stronger that will wake you up and get your taste buds ready for a great brunch, try the following. It's the old Kahlua and coffee but with a twist.

Shopping List

3 cups cold coffee

3 oz Kahlua

3 oz vodka

1 oz brandy

3 oz cream

Preparation

1. Put all ingredients into a shaker with ice and shake well

2. Pour over ice and serve sparingly

Notes

NOTES

One thing you know in advance of sitting down to a meal on Jim and Nan's cottage porch is that the food, no matter how simple, will be delicious and somehow original. The semi panoramic view across Crystal Lake, just a few yards from where you sit, provides a serene backdrop and surreptitiously instills the impression that you have known the place for your whole life, even if you are a relative newcomer. And that impression is always reinforced by the congenial and eclectic company that shows up to join you, invited or just dropping by!

Tim Richardson

Index of Recipes

Summer

In the spring, the sun sets over the northwest corner of Crystal Lake. As the summer progresses, the sunsets move toward the southwest corner of the lake, still just as spectacular with their hues of red, orange and pink bouncing off the clouds, but as they move, it's a reminder that summer is passing. In the spring, the delicate and spongy morel mushrooms with their deep earthy flavor bring the promise of another summer full of warm sunny days, seemingly endless, and perfect for swimming, boating, biking, books on the beach, and meals on the porch. But mostly they bring the promise of friends and family sharing in all the joys of summer, their laughter mixing with the sounds of the wind in the birch and pine trees, the waves on the beach, the bees in the wildflower patches, and the boats on the lake. The morel mushrooms don't last long, but we hardly notice with the tender asparagus and sweet strawberries, blackberries, and raspberries coming into season. The Fourth of July may mark the height of the season for most, but for me, it's the plump cherries, zucchini, and tomatoes that tell me summer is in full swing. Dinners of lake trout and white fish on the grill with new potatoes and corn-on-the-cob elicit stories of embellished golf games, impossibly long bike rides, and the requisite fish stories. But there always comes the time when I notice that the trillium, baby's breath, and daisies have given way to the Black-eyed Susans and Queen Anne's Lace. The cherries and peaches are gone and the crispness of the apples seems to mimic the coolness that can be detected beneath the breeze. Sandy beach towels are left in car trunks, bicycles lean up against cottages, docks start to disappear from the lake, and the smell of wood-burning fireplaces is in the air. Lights give a yellow glow to the porch as conversations over salmon dinners start to include talk of new school years, politics, and work projects. I take it all in, still enjoying the warmth given off by the camaraderie of life-long friends but feeling a tug of melancholy creeping in as I wrap my sweater a little tighter around me. I know, no matter what the calendar says, the year ends with summer.